Religion and Literature

RELIGION AND LITERATURE

Helen Gardner

OXFORD NEW YORK
OXFORD UNIVERSITY PRESS

Oxford University Press, Walton Street, Oxford OX2 6DP
London Glasgow New York Toronto
Delhi Bombay Calcutta Madras Karachi
Kuala Lumpur Singapore Hong Kong Tokyo
Nairobi Dar es Salaam Cape Town
Melbourne Auckland
and associated companies in
Beirut Berlin Ibadan Mexico City Nicosia

Oxford is a trade mark of Oxford University Press

First published 1971

First issued as an Oxford University Press paperback 1983

British Library Cataloguing in Publication Data

Gardner, Helen, 1908–
Religion and literature.
1. Religion and literature   2. English literature—
History and criticism
I. Title
820'.9'3   PR145
ISBN 0-19-812824-X.

Printed in Great Britain
at the University Press, Oxford
by Eric Buckley
Printer to the University

Preface

The two sets of lectures published together here are, I hope, complementary. The first set, on 'Religion and Tragedy', originated in four lectures given in the University of Bristol in the spring of 1965. These were lectures for an annual series in which scholars were asked to speak on some topic involving the relation of their subject to the Christian Faith. The invitation to give the second set of T. S. Eliot Memorial Lectures in the University of Kent at Canterbury in 1968 gave me an opportunity to return to the topic, expand and revise my first attempt to discuss it, and give it a wider application. It had suggested itself to me in the first place because of uneasiness I felt at some of Eliot's pronouncements on Shakespeare, and from thinking over his many attempts to relate his criticism of literature to his beliefs. I thought I should best honour his memory by taking up questions to which he often recurred and which plainly teased and troubled him, even though they are questions which do not admit of solutions.

The second set is also connected with T. S. Eliot, who some years ago asked me to compile an anthology of religious verse. When I was invited to give the Ewing Lectures in California in the spring of 1966 I had begun work for this and was much occupied with problems of definition and selection. I was struck by a parallel problem to the problem of the rarity of tragedy, which I had discussed the year before: the quantity and quality of religious verse in some periods compared with its paucity and general feebleness in others. In these lectures I defined religious poetry strictly, as poetry expressing religious commitment; and attempted to discuss the different forms available to religious poets in different ages. In the first set of lectures the topic is a wider one and less well defined: the relation of the religious thought of his age to the imagination of a poet concerned with the whole of life, and not with the restricted area of religious belief and religious experience. The two sets of lectures thus start from different ends; but they are both concerned with changes in literary and religious sensibility and their interaction. For, as Eliot said: 'Religious feeling varies naturally from country to country, and from age to age, just as poetic feeling does; the feeling varies, even when the belief, the doctrine remains the same' (*On Poetry and Poets*, 1957, p. 25).

I have to thank the University of Bristol for the invitation to lecture there in 1965, and the University of Kent for honouring me with the invitation to deliver the T. S. Eliot Memorial Lectures and for kind hospitality in Eliot College. My first happy visit to the University of California at Los Angeles was in 1954, when I spent a semester there as Visiting Professor. My second, even happier, since it is more delightful to see old friends again than to make new ones, was in the spring of 1966 to deliver the Ewing Lectures, founded by the generosity of Professor and Mrs. Majl Ewing. . . .

I have to thank Mrs. Willa Muir, Mr. W. H. Auden, the Literary Executors of Louis MacNeice, and Messrs. Faber and Faber for permission to quote 'The Angel and the girl are met' on p. 139, the lullaby from *For the Time Being* on p. 141, and for the extract from *Autumn Journal* on pp. 44 and 45.

HELEN GARDNER

Oxford,
1971

For this reprinting I have made no changes in the text, except for the correction of misprints.

HELEN GARDNER

Oxford,
1983

Contents

RELIGION AND TRAGEDY

The T. S. Eliot Memorial Lectures

Delivered at Eliot College in the University of Kent
at Canterbury, October 1968

I

Concepts of Tragedy

These lectures were founded in memory of T. S. Eliot to be given on an appropriate topic. It seemed to me that I should choose a theme that had bearing on his work as poet and critic, that the subject should be a wide one, and the lectures more exploratory than informative. Re-reading Eliot's criticism today one is struck by the persistence with which he recurred to certain perennial problems in criticism. From the influential essay on 'Shakespeare and the Stoicism of Seneca' onwards he returned again and again to the twin problems it raised: how far 'belief proper enters into the activity of a great poet *qua* poet' and the relation of a poet's 'thought' or his 'philosophy' to the thought of his time. Eliot's polemical purpose in the essay is clear. He was arguing to defend the autonomy of poetry, to make clear that the activity of writing a poem is not the same as the activities of worshipping, praying, preaching, or writing a philosophical treatise or a theological work. He wanted to protect poetry from those who would make its main interest autobiographical or confessional, and from those who would find its value in a 'philosophy' or a 'view of life' encapsulated in a poem to be extracted from it for use. He went so far in this essay as to say that the poet, far from thinking for himself or believing, merely 'uses' a theory which fuses with his 'initial emotional impulse' to make poetry. Contrasting Dante with Shakespeare, he declared that Dante's advantage over Shakespeare, if indeed he had the advantage, lay not in his being a believer, whereas Shakespeare probably was not, but in his good fortune in having a theory to make use of which was the work of a great and noble mind, whereas the less fortunate Shakespeare had to make do with 'the thought of persons far inferior to himself'. He summed up by saying, 'You can hardly say that Dante believed or did not believe the Thomist philosophy: you can hardly say that Shakespeare did or did not believe the mixed and muddled scepticism of the Renaissance.' Both were concerned with the true business of the poet: 'to express the greatest emotional intensity of his time based on whatever his time happened to think'.

It is impossible to rest content with this conception of the poet as merely using a theory current in his age which meshes with his emotional impulses, as intellectually irresponsible and concerned only with truth of feeling. Eliot moved a long way from it in later discussions and it is patently inadequate to his own practice and achievement as a poet and to his relation to his age. It also conflicts with the statements of many great poets, who have believed they were saying something of great moment, and with the testimony of generations of readers, who have found in great poetry not merely images of life but images that are interpretative. Throughout the ages men have found the interpretative function of the poet pre-eminently discharged by the tragic poets, and have regarded tragedy as presenting in its image of what men do and suffer an image that shows us the workings of laws in human life, revealing truth about the 'nature of things' as well as truths about the natures of men. I thought therefore that I might approach indirectly the problem of 'meaning' with which Eliot was always so much concerned by some reflections on tragedy and the relation of religion and tragedy in fifth-century Athens and Elizabethan London.

It used to be said as axiomatic that while Greek Tragedy is soaked in religious conceptions and concerned with the relation of man to the gods, Shakespearian Tragedy is agnostic and concerned with the relation of man to man. Many writers on tragedy have indeed affirmed, and some still do, that there is a deep discord between the tragic and the Christian view of man and his destiny, and that there is some doubt whether 'tragedy be at all possible under the protection and in the light of revealed religion'.[1] But in recent years we have seen many attempts to Christianize Shakespeare's tragedies, and in place of a Shakespeare building his tragedies on the 'mixed and muddle scepticism of the Renaissance' we have been presented with a Shakespeare who built them on the orthodox pietisms of Elizabethan England. It is by no means only, or even conspicuously, those who would themselves claim 'the honourable style of Christian' who have thus attempted to make Shakespeare's tragedies the expression of the commonplaces of sixteenth-century theology. The enterprise has often been conducted by persons to whom Christianity is a historical phenomenon and not a present way of life. It has been part of the attempt to arrive at objective criteria of interpretation and escape the dangers of subjectivity, to rescue Shakespeare from those who would kidnap him and drag him by force into a later age. Neither view seems to me satisfactory, and I wish to discuss the relation of a poet's 'thought' to the thought of his age by considering in what senses, if any, Shakespeare's tragedies can legitimately be regarded as 'Christian Tragedy'. There was a further reason which made me choose this topic. Eliot himself made two striking attempts at writing tragedies which should not be Shakespearian *pastiche* but should render the matter of tragedy in a modern approximation to its original ancient form. Both *Murder in the Cathedral* and *The Family Reunion* are moving and powerful plays. Neither has, I think, an effect really comparable with the effect of tragedy. I do not think this was because Eliot was a Christian but because, to use his own word, conditions were 'unpropitious'.[2] Tragedy is a rare phenomenon, unlike comedy which flourishes in every generation. It appears to be possible only at certain brief periods. At other times, attempts to write tragedy result in plays that are drearily imitative of great works of the past and have no life of their own, or in plays that although powerful lack the

[1] W. Macneile Dixon, *Tragedy* (1924), 9.
[2] *There is only the fight to recover what has been lost*
And found and lost again and again: and now, under conditions
That seem unpropitious.
                                        East Coker, V.

[*15*]

peculiar power of tragedy. I want in my last lecture to suggest some parallels in the sixteenth century to conditions that have been suggested as explanatory of the rise of Attic Tragedy in the fifth century B.C. and then to consider relations between drama in our own day and the religious consciousness of this century.

In recent years there has been a strong reaction against discussion of the concept of 'Tragedy', and even more against attempts to characterize 'the tragic sense' or 'the tragic vision'. The very phrases sound old-fashioned and rather stuffy. Greek Tragedy, it is said, does not exist: there are only a number of extant Greek Tragedies. 'Shakespearian Tragedy' was invented by Bradley: there are only a number of plays, differing very widely from each other, which are loosely grouped together under the title of 'Shakespearian Tragedies'. Discussion of 'Tragedy' or of 'Shakespearian Tragedy' is discussion of a critical abstraction which is a hindrance to understanding of the plays that are forced to conform with it. It can also blind us to the merits and interest of other plays which we measure against our definition and decide are not 'fully tragic'. There is a good deal of truth and good sense in this view. It is also natural, in an age in which the whole notion of literary 'kinds' has ceased to have any meaning for poets and dramatists, that critics should feel impatient at discussion of a 'kind', and at generalizations which, of necessity, obscure the individuality of works of art. For a main critical preoccupation today is to discover the proper response to individual works.

Yet I cannot accept that 'Tragedy' is a 'pseudo-subject for discussion'; or that the question 'What is Tragedy?', or what makes us willing to give this title to certain works and deny it to others, is an unreal question. Questions to which precise, unambiguous, and universally satisfactory answers can be given are not the only questions worth asking. In literary criticism questions that resist final solution and are reopened again and again are often seminal and give incidental rewards. However much debate there may be about this or that play, there is a corpus of drama whose claim to the title of tragedy nobody would dispute. To the question 'What is a Tragedy?' a preliminary answer can at once be given, on the

model of W. P. Ker's answer to the question 'What is a ballad?':
'A Tragedy is *Oedipus Rex*, *Antigone*, *Hamlet*, *King Lear* or *Phèdre*.'
And at once we can add that such a list shows that 'Tragedy' is a
term of honour and more than a description of a certain literary
'kind'. In giving such a list we are naming masterpieces of art. To
speak of 'great tragedy' is really a tautology. Tragedy that is not
'great' is not tragedy, but 'failed tragedy'. Again, I do not think
we can dismiss as a pseudo-question a question that has presented
itself as a true question to many profound and sensitive minds.
Their answers, however partial or unsatisfactory we may find
them, have one thing in common for all their variety. They agree
in assuming that men derive from tragedies some 'new acquist of
true experience': that they find in tragedy, beyond its adequacy as
a true image of human life, an interpretation of life that echoes or
chimes with their own most serious reflections. And further, however impatient we may feel with well-worn phrases such as the
'tragic vision' or the 'tragic sense' and however strongly we declare
that we are interested in tragedies and not in some vague concept
of 'the tragic', we cannot ignore the extension of the adjective. It
was very early extended from works of art of a particular kind to
events and episodes in actual life resembling those on which the
tragic poets based their plays. More striking is its extension in art
beyond the confines of drama. It was only a small extension when
Richardson applied it to narrative fiction and declared that in
Clarissa he was attempting something 'of the Tragic Kind'. It was
a larger extension when it was applied to the visual arts which,
being static, lack that movement to a promised end which seems
an essential element in tragedies. If plot is the soul of tragedy in
what sense are paintings and sculptures spoken of as tragic? Most
striking is the extension of the term to music, the most abstract of
the arts, presenting no 'image of life'. But we do not feel it absurd
that Brahms should have called a piece of music 'The Tragic
Overture', or that critics should speak of Beethoven's last
Quartet and of the C Sharp Minor Quartet as tragic works,
possessing the same power as tragedies have to elevate painful
emotions and in doing so to calm them.

[*17*]

Strictly speaking, there are no tragedies in real life. A tragedy is a work of art and is thus designed to give pleasure. Events are not in themselves tragic. They are calamitous, shocking, pitiful, or terrible, but not tragic until the imagination has worked on them. In arousing in us pity, horror, or dismay, they frequently demand action from us. If disaster has overtaken a friend or neighbour we must go to his help: if there has been an earthquake or a flood, we ought, if we ourselves cannot go and help, at least to send a cheque to a relief fund. And when there is nothing we can do, when a friend has committed a crime, or perhaps taken his own life in despair, we feel a turmoil of emotions, bafflement at the motives that led to such an act, some sense of guilt perhaps at having failed in friendship, uneasy feelings of misgiving—'There, but for the grace of God, go I'—but certainly there is no pleasure in feeling such emotions. When it is a stranger whose misfortunes we read of in the newspaper, or when we watch some horror on the television screen, or an interview with someone involved in greatly distressing circumstances, we may feel rather ashamed of our interest in the afflictions or dreadful actions of some fellow-man, and of our curiosity. If we feel any pleasure in hearing or reading or seeing such things, it is a pleasure we have some shame in feeling, or at least in confessing to feeling, if we are persons who hope we may regard ourselves as civilized. We call such curiosity morbid, and stigmatize as self-indulgent, and worse, the desire to find in the calamities of real life a source for the stimulation of the emotions. Even so there are both in actual life, and even more in history, events and stories of which we feel immediately that they are more than material for tragedy, but are incipiently tragic, more than halfway towards assuming tragic form and, therefore, by a legitimate extension of the word referred to as tragedies. This is particularly so in history, where the imaginations of men have worked upon the stuff of experience to give it shape, so that certain events, certain stories, certain lives have taken a meaningful pattern. We call them tragic or even speak of them as tragedies not only because they are the kind of events and stories the tragic writer chooses, but because we see in them a disposition of events and a relation of motive to event which has the irony characteristic of tragedy. And to many historical persons the perspective of history and the idealizing habit of the human imagination have given singularity or greatness, the exceptional human qualities we associate with the personages of tragedy.

Why, faintly in historic events and events in which we have no personal concern, and strongly in works of art which deal with such events, we feel pleasure in contemplating what in actuality would disturb and distress us, value most highly those in which the matter is most shocking and distressing, and are disappointed if the distress is mitigated in the conclusion and the persons escape from the net woven by the plot, or are saved from the catastrophe we have seen impending, is a question that has exercised philosophers rather than literary critics. It did not appear to interest Aristotle. He merely remarks, as facts of experience, that the best situation for a tragedy is the one in which the 'deed of horror' (as Bywater translated *to deinon*) takes place among close relations, members of a family, and that the worst kind of plot is when a man in full knowledge is about to perform a terrible deed and then draws back. That is, the worst situation in real life, when 'a man's foes are of his own household', is the best in tragedy, and a turn of events that we should welcome in actuality—that, at the last moment, a man repents and refrains from the evil he had planned—is a disappointment to spectators or readers of tragedy. We should feel cheated rather than relieved if Medea abandoned her intention of murdering her children, or if Macbeth followed the example of the Thane of Cawdor, repented, confessed his treasons, and accepted his punishment. Aristotle is content to state as a fact that the more distressing the events the better the tragedy will be. As far as I know, the first person to ponder on the oddity of this was Augustine in a famous passage in the *Confessions* where he puzzled over his intense susceptibility to stage plays in his youth and asked why he should have enjoyed 'sights full of the images of my own miseries and of fuel to my own fire'. And he asks:

Why is it that man desires to be afflicted at the sight of grievous
and tragical things which he himself would not wish to suffer.
Yet for all that, as a spectator he wishes to feel sorrow at them,
and indeed this very sorrow is his pleasure. What is this but a
miserable madness? For every man is the more affected by these
things the less free he is of such affections; although when a
man himself suffers we call it misery, and when he has a fellow-
feeling for others we call it compassion.[1] But what kind of compassion can there be for fictitious and theatrical actions? For
the auditor is not moved to give help, but invited merely to
grieve, and the more he grieves the more he applauds the author
of these representations. And if these human calamities, either
long past or else wholly invented, are so handled that the spectator is not grieved, he leaves the theatre, disgusted and critical;
but if he is grieved he sits intently to the end, and is happy and
pleased.[2]

Augustine speaks as a moralist who believes that our passions are
given to us not to be indulged but as spurs to our wills: our
capacity to feel distress at the sufferings of others should incite us
to acts of mercy. Centuries later Hume, echoing Augustine's words
though assuming an even more overtly emotional audience, looks
at the matter as a psychologist:

It seems an unaccountable pleasure which the spectators of a
well-written tragedy receive from sorrow, terror, anxiety, and
other passions that are themselves disagreeable and uneasy.
The more they are touched and affected, the more are they
delighted with the spectacle; and as soon as the uneasy passions
cease to operate, the piece is at an end. One scene of full joy
and contentment and security is the utmost that any composition of this kind can bear; and it is sure always to be the concluding one. If in the texture of the piece there be interwoven
any scenes of satisfaction, they afford only faint gleams of
pleasure, which are thrown in by way of variety, and in order
to plunge the actors into deeper distress by means of that
contrast and disappointment. The whole art of the poet is
employed in rousing and supporting the compassion and indignation, the anxiety and resentment of his audience. They are
pleased in proportion as they are afflicted, and never are so

[1] It is impossible to bring out the pun in *miseria* and *misericordia*.
[2] *Confessions*, III. ii.

happy as when they employ tears, sobs, and cries to give vent to their sorrows and relieve their hearts swollen with the tenderest sympathy and compassion.

Some of the answers given to this question of why we enjoy tragedies do little credit to human nature, and those based on Aristotle's medical metaphor of *catharsis*, by which we go to the theatre as to a clinic to have our psychic balance adjusted, hardly seem to explain why persons who are not obviously over-emotional, neurotic, or psychologically unbalanced enjoy trage-dies. This is the fundamental paradox of tragic art and the problem that first engaged what Hume called 'the few critics who have had some tincture of philosophy'; that its pleasure is a painful pleasure. If pleasure seems today too weak a word, and delight and enjoy-ment also have not the force needed, it can be said that tragedy elevates the spirits rather than depresses them, or that it satisfies us though its matter is all those elements in human life that make it unsatisfactory: human suffering endured and inflicted, which means suffering that includes guilt; changes and chances that destroy happiness; intolerable dilemmas in which either course of action must be equally disastrous or offensive to the conscience; the destructive force of malice. These permanent elements in human experience are isolated from all the blessed day-to-day businesses of living which in actual life help us to bear them, and they are shown as irremediable, not to be got round. In comedy we are shown a world in which there may be disappointments and sorrows; but they are shown as things to be lived with. Happiness is possible if we do not demand too much, and if we accept that life is a mingled yarn. If we will learn to live and let live, joy will come in the morning. Some have held that tragedies exist to impress on us the same lesson: be moderate, observe the mean, be well balanced, normal and inoffensive. The wind strikes the lofty tree: it passes harmlessly over the lowly shrub. Be a shrub: see what happens to trees. The personages of tragedy are, in this view, warnings to us, examples of pride, arrogance, obstinacy, and of failures to understand their own natures and the nature of the world. We may learn from these 'over-reachers' to bear ourselves modestly and humbly, recognize the limitations of our human condition, and make no great demands upon life. This lesson can easily be deduced from many tragedies; but to regard tragedy as essentially a dramatic cautionary tale is to evacuate tragedy of what is a main source of that painful pleasure that puzzled Augustine, the passionate sympathy with which he owns he followed the joys and sorrows of 'guilty lovers'. The figures of tragedy arouse passionate concern; their fates are terrible because they impress upon us so strong a sense of their exceptional value. One has to return to Aristotle's observation that they are 'better' than we are, though precisely what sense, or senses, we are to give to 'better' remains a question. And here is the second paradox of tragedy: that many of the figures who call out such a profound response of sympathy, admiration and awe commit acts that are repugnant and that would in life inhibit sympathy with their perpetrators. For tragedy is as much concerned with the crimes of men as with their sufferings; it could indeed be argued that tragedy is more concerned with guilt than with sorrow. But even in tragedies in which the main persons are 'more sinned against than sinning', or sin in ignorance, or madness, they do not arouse impatience or a sense of superiority in those who watch their sufferings or their errors. Critics may point out how awkward, obstinate and self-righteous Antigone is, and censure the irascible and unaccommodating Lear who will not accept that 'age is unnecessary'; but in the imagination of the world, and to spectators in the theatre, Antigone's heroic solitude and Lear's heroic endurance inhibit criticism. Tragedies do not evoke in the theatre either the hissing or applause that is the response to melodrama, or laughter at the recognition of human folly, or the soft smiling that arises from the exposure of those we feel we understand better than they understand themselves. The sense of human greatness, integrity, or nobility, and of the capacities of human nature, suspends moral judgment. As we take pleasure in the representation of things that in actual life we should find it painful and distressing to watch, so we sympathize and admire persons whose acts would in life shock and repel us, or, at best, irritate us and provoke criticism.

To Hume the main problem of tragedy was the problem why it should please. He found the source of tragic pleasure to lie in eloquence which delights us so greatly that it overmasters painful feelings, and, being the predominant emotion, absorbs into itself the strength of painful emotions which are themselves a spur to eloquence and its justification. The philosophers and philosophic critics of the nineteenth century were unable to rest content with a theory that found the pleasure of tragedy to lie in our response to aesthetic expressiveness, and appeared indifferent to what the poet says in admiration for the lovely way he says it. For the theory seemed to reduce the poet to the level of the orator. The new romantic concepts of the poet as not merely the 'interpreter of the best and sagest things' but as the explorer of experience, and of poetry as 'being more philosophic than history' in a far wider sense than Aristotle intended, transferred the discussion from the psychology of the audience to the creative mind of the poet. The persistent attempts to define tragedy and discuss not its formal aspects but the 'vision of tragedy', however contradictory, show a common recognition of tragedy as deeply serious, revealing important truth about the nature of human life. Our pleasure in it cannot, it is felt, be sufficiently explained by Aristotle's statement that men delight in imitation and in works of imitation and that our pleasure in learning and in recognition outweighs the disagreeable elements in the thing imitated, or in Hume's stress on our delight in eloquence. New words are found to give some deeper content to the word 'pleasure'. Tragedy satisfies, tragedy illuminates, tragedy exalts, tragedy consoles. Attempts are made to formulate a vision of life discovered in the works of the tragic poets and to discover why this should satisfy or console. They are made in the terms of the writer's own philosophy. But I do not think we can neglect the nineteenth-century discussions on tragedy and its power to satisfy and reveal truth about the human condition because they appear so long after the works they praise and interpret were written, and are couched in terms and employ concepts the authors of those works and the critics of their day did not and indeed could not employ; or because they are couched in terms and use concepts we should not ourselves use. Nor are they necessarily invalidated by the fact that the age in which theories of tragedy most proliferated was an age which notably failed in its attempts to create tragedies. They are a witness to the extraordinary vitality of great works of art, which perpetually invite formulation and re-formulation of the values men find in them, and live by this process of interpretation and re-interpretation in successive ages, even while they resist it, and become the richer for it.

From the beginning, in all discussions of tragedy, one note is always struck: that tragedy includes, or reconciles, or preserves in tension, contraries. Aristotle said that the distinctive tragic emotions were pity and fear and implied that both must be present to secure the tragic effect. He uses them so constantly together as almost to suggest that they must be felt simultaneously, as if there were not two emotions, either pity or fear, but a single emotion: pity-and-fear. Some later writers have attempted to find a single term, such as 'the tragic qualm', to express this feeling that is more than pity plus fear or pity alternating with fear. To judge by common usage these are contrary feelings. Pity is a warm feeling, fear a cold one: we feel a 'warm rush of pity', but a 'chilling sense of fear'. Pity is out-going and self-forgetful: fear shrinks back and is self-regarding. Aristotle also declared that tragedy should show an action that is complete, and completion implies a design. But when we attempt to analyse the design of a tragedy we are often hard put to it to assert what is the dominant line that creates the pattern, and when we turn to reading critics we can find diametrically opposed readings.[1] To one writer it is the logic of human wills and passions that creates the design: to another the over-riding power of fate or destiny. But each has to own the presence of the other element. Those who see primarily a clash of human wills have to own that into the plot that the passions or the self-

[1] It seems difficult to believe that Hegel and Schopenhauer had been reading the same play when after reading Hegel on the *Antigone*, we find Schopenhauer classing it as one of the plays in which great misfortune is brought about by means of 'a character of extraordinary wickedness', and ranking Creon with Richard III and Iago.

betrayals of men spin there intrude chance accidents and painful turns of event that no prudence could possibly have foreseen: that 'our thoughts are ours, their ends none of our own'. On the other hand, those who see the dominant element in the pattern, the line that creates the design, in the workings of fate, ironically frustrating the wills of men to bring about a destined end, cannot refuse responsibility to the wills and passions of men. They have to acknowledge that the movement of tragic plots towards finality is not a relentless movement, an irresistible force that sweeps men away and carries them helpless but protesting to their doom. Tragedy does not show man as 'master of his fate' and 'captain of his soul': but neither does it show

> *helpless man, in ignorance sedate,*
> *Roll darkling down the torrent of his fate.*[1]

Its matter is made up of both what men do and what men suffer. Its pattern is woven out of the action and the suffering. This tension in tragic plots by which man appears as architect of his fate and its victim was given a metaphysical and religious interpretation in a famous passage in *Murder in the Cathedral*:

> *acting is suffering*
> *And suffering is action. Neither does the actor suffer*
> *Nor the patient act. But both are fixed*
> *In an eternal action, an eternal patience*
> *To which all must consent that it may be willed*
> *And which all must suffer that they may will it,*
> *That the pattern may subsist, for the pattern is the action*
> *And the suffering.*

Many have held that the prime element in the satisfaction tragedy affords is that it presents an unintelligible world made intelligible: that though it shows us a world apparently full of mutability and irrationality, it shows us in the end a world that has meaning and rationality and is governed by laws. Some with crudity and others with subtlety have attempted to find in tragedy

[1] Samuel Johnson, *The Vanity of Human Wishes*, ll. 345–6.

a justification of the universe as ultimately making sense. Such efforts are unfashionable today, and much mocked at. But they cannot be disregarded and perhaps future and happier ages than ours will find the desire of many in our day to find in tragedy the vision of a universe that makes no sense at all as much a subject for mockery. The most subtle and I suppose the most influential of such theories is Hegel's, who sees in tragedy the representation of the clash of two ideals, each noble and worthy, but incompatible. Our satisfaction arises from the demonstration of the inevitable one-sidedness of human ideals. It is difficult to see why this conclusion should satisfy, and even more difficult to apply this analysis of the tragic *agon* to extant tragedies. Hegel's account of the *Antigone* on which he rests his theory seems painfully in contradiction to the testimony of the ages which Shelley voiced when he said: 'Every man in some previous existence has been in love with an Antigone.' If the gods do not love Antigone, so much the worse for the gods. Bradley attempted to widen Hegel's theory which he thought left much out of account and was inadequate to Shakespearian Tragedy. He felt Hegel seriously diminished the element of suffering and exaggerated the element of reconciliation in one way while rating it too low in another. He added to the idea of conflict in the 'ethical substance' of the universe the idea of conflict in the 'spiritual substance' of individual man, and to the idea of conflict as the essential of tragedy he added the notion that the conflict entails waste. He thought that Hegel underrated the part played by 'moral evil rather than defect'. But even so, for all his tenderer heart, Bradley remained an optimist, finding 'the element of reconciliation in the catastrophe' to be 'strengthened by recognition of the part played by evil in bringing it about; because our sense that the ultimate power cannot endure the presence of such evil is implicitly the sense that this power is at least more closely allied with good'.[1] The deduction seems illicit. It is surely very questionable whether an 'ultimate power' so impatient at the presence of Iago that it removes him at the cost

[1] See the lecture on 'Hegel's Theory of Tragedy' in *Oxford Lectures on Poetry* (1917), p. 85.

of the destruction of Othello and of Desdemona appears at all 'closely allied with good'.

Others, less subtle than Hegel and less sensitive than Bradley, have attempted to justify the scheme of things by extravagant and illicit extensions of the Aristotelian concept of *hamartia*, a word that has suffered as remarkable a development as his other term *catharsis*. What was to Aristotle a vital element in the plot—that the catastrophe should arise from some mistake, an error of judgment, and that the sufferer should not be pre-eminently virtuous or just, so that his fate should not outrage us—has been transformed into the 'tragic flaw': some natural moral obliquity in the tragic hero, a defect of character or temperament, which reconciles us to his fate as being not wholly unmerited. If we can hardly claim that the laws of the universe are wholly just, at least we may say that the nature of things has some rationality. How things are to some extent corresponds to how things ought to be. The more determined and fanatical upholders of this view, in their anxiety to justify the universe, go so far as virtually to deny that any of the sufferers in a tragedy is innocent. Gervinus, though mocked, still rides in article after article in which the errors and misdoings of major and minor characters alike are shown as the causes of catastrophe. Any weakness or peccadillo is good enough. Desdemona disobeys her father—off with her head: Ophelia obeys hers—off with her head. It is an eccentric form of justice that metes out the same punishment to errors and crimes alike and odd that it should be thought consoling to conceive of the universe as ruled by the Queen of Hearts. The more moderate of the moralists confine their attempts to prove that it is the justice of the close that satisfies us to concentration on the central figure, the tragic hero, and discover in his 'fatal flaw' the cause of his downfall. Owning that chance, accident, circumstances, and the malice of others all play their part, and that the hero in bringing down ruin on himself involves the innocent in his fate, they find the potent element in the design to lie in the hero's own character, and try to persuade us that the end satisfies us by showing that his fate was not wholly unjust.

This view, that our satisfaction at the close is a moral satisfaction, that we recognize and acknowledge, though with pain, that the hero has brought his doom on himself, has been powerfully attacked by what one must call the 'Glasgow School'. Beginning with Macneile Dixon, whose book on Tragedy, though written in a style that today seems at times arch and at other times florid, I find sympathetic, continued by his colleague J. S. Smart in a well-known essay,[1] and by their pupil Peter Alexander in his lectures on *Hamlet, Father and Son* (1955), the Glasgow School has consistently challenged the view that the secret of tragedy's power to satisfy us lies in its demonstration of human failure making human suffering explicable. *Hamlet* as the 'tragedy of a man who could not make up his mind'; *Othello* as the tragedy of egoism and lack of self-knowledge; *King Lear* as the tragedy of unbridled will—these critical commonplaces are repugnant to them. They insist that it is the virtues of the tragic figures that interest us. They challenge Aristotle's view that the sight of a good man suffering unmerited misfortune is not tragic; and assert that the attempt to show tragedy as justifying the scheme of things, and proving that Fate or Destiny is moral, runs completely counter to what tragedies present, bears no relation to what men actually experience when viewing tragedy, and is an outrage on our moral sense. Moral values are, in their view, embodied in the figures of tragedy and not in the fates that befall them. Tragedy, they declare, celebrates virtues of which the world is not worthy. It displays qualities that are the glory of human nature: courage, fidelity, strength to endure, the passion to know and understand, and the passion to secure justice. It shows them as not necessarily serving good ends, or as bringing happiness or success—on the contrary it is these virtues rather than faults that are shown as the causes of worldly disaster. They are shown as beautiful and to be honoured for themselves, the more so because they are unrewarded. To these critics tragedy vindicates the universe only in the sense that it displays a universe that provides the opportunity for the existence, and the exercise, of virtue. And yet, though we may feel the

[1] In *Essays and Studies by Members of the English Association* (1922).

strength and the justice of this assault on Bradley's over-emphasis on the 'tragic flaw', and respond to this generous indignation at the grim moralizings of the school of Gervinus, there come from the choruses in ancient tragedy, from bystanders in modern, and even from the mouths of tragic victims themselves assertions that demand we should see some nexus between a man's sowing and his reaping.

Those philosophers who are less optimistic about the course of worldly things and feel therefore no compulsion to pin blame on man for his sorrows, misfortunes, and errors, Schopenhauer and Nietzsche, do not outrage our feelings by failing to recognize the appalling element in tragedy: that it displays calamities that can by no moral standard at all be conceived of as deserved. In Schopenhauer's view the sole essential in tragedy is the representation of 'a great misfortune'. The end of tragedy is to display the 'terrible side of life' and by so doing give us 'a significant hint of the nature of the world and of existence'. It shows 'the strife of the will with itself' raised to such a height that it has 'a *quieting* effect', producing 'resignation, the surrender not merely of life, but of the very will to live'. We see in tragedies, 'the noblest men, after long conflict and suffering, at last renounce the ends they have so keenly followed, and all the pleasures of life for ever, or else freely and joyfully surrender life itself'. The elevation of soul that the spectator feels at the close of a tragedy comes from the fact that tragedy releases us from our painful attachment to life and gives us a taste of the bliss of resignation and renunciation. 'Thus the summons to turn away the will from life remains the true tendency of tragedy, the ultimate end of the intentional exhibition of the suffering of humanity.' For it is not for his own individual sins that the tragic hero atones, but for original sin, that is the 'crime of existence itself':

> *For the greatest crime of man*
> *Is that he was born.*

Schopenhauer is the first writer, as far as I know, to erect a theory of tragedy that boldly disregards what virtually all great tragedies show, in order to concentrate on what he declares should be their effect on the spectator. He admits candidly that the ancients inadequately grasped the true conception of the tragic and that the spirit of resignation does not reign in classical tragedy. And when he comes to modern tragedy, he finds Goethe's *Clavigo* a more perfect example of the highest kind of tragedy than *Hamlet*, and reserves his highest praise for Bellini's opera *Norma*, where the change of the will of the hero to resignation and exaltation is 'distinctly indicated by the quietness which is suddenly introduced into the music'.

It is impossible to argue with Schopenhauer for he has cut the ground from under our feet by anticipating the objection that neither in Greek tragedies nor in most modern do the heroes in the end throw in the sponge, give up the struggle, recognize the game was not worth the candle, and 'embrace the darkness as a bride'. His theory grasps that it is the finality of tragedy that satisfies us— that the end brings peace because all is over, the story is complete, 'the rest is silence', 'ther is namore to seye'. It does not explain the fascination of the struggle and why surely the majority of us do not feel as we watch impatience that the hero will not recognize that the world is not worth his care. If the end only satisfies us by showing that all that went before was worthless, and that 'effort and expectation and desire' are pernicious follies, it is difficult to explain what has held us enthralled for the two or more hours before. The notion that the lesson of tragedy, to use words Freud used of *King Lear*, is to teach us 'to renounce life and renounce love and make friends with the necessity of dying', though it recognizes the omnipresence of the unhappy ending, and even more of death, in modern as opposed to ancient tragedy, does not do justice to what tragedy as a whole displays, the sense of life as potentially glorious. It neglects all we include in our sense of the heroic.

This is fully recognized by Nietzsche in the most thrilling and beautiful of all theories of tragedy. Nietzsche saw in tragedy the fusion of two types of art, the Dionysian and the Apollonian. Tragedy, he claimed, arose out of the chorus, the Dionysian dithy-

ramb, echoing the awful sadness of things and the horror of existence; but this begets its opposite, the beautiful, individual figures
of Apollonian art, a sublime spectacle which is in the end merged
in the deeper reality of the Dionysian wisdom. Nietzsche's is one
of the few theories of tragedy that grants us the beauty of tragedy
and the tragic figures, sees tragedy as 'gorgeous tragedy', allows
for our poignant sense of the value of what is destroyed and the
strength of our desire that it should not be destroyed. Tragedy is
to him 'the art of metaphysical comfort', reconciling us to life by
showing it as a sublime spectacle, and to the universe as work of
unmoral art. But, again, when we turn from this beautiful and
heady theory to tragedies as they have been written, and as we
read them, it seems impossible to evacuate them thus of moral
values and moral concern. The original tragic chorus may have
been a group of worshippers expressing an inarticulate sense of
the world's sorrow that only music can ultimately render; on the
other hand it very well may not. The title of Nietzsche's book, *The
Birth of Tragedy*, allies it with many fascinating late-nineteenth-
century speculations on the origin of this and that: theories about
primitive religion and primitive society, thought up by people
who had never observed a primitive people, forever unprovable
and now looking more and more implausible. They derive from
the great revolution in human thought which made men turn
away from the classic notion that the essential nature of an object
is best grasped by studying it in its ideal perfection, or at least in its
full development, to the romantic notion that its essential nature
is to be found in its primitive form. Where the primitive form was
not available for observation, it had to be deduced. But when we
turn from Nietzsche's theory to extant ancient tragedies, we find
that it is largely in the choruses that we find articulated the moral
questions and concerns that Nietzsche set aside; and on the faces
of the beautiful figures of Apollonian art we see the marks of the
deepest suffering. Nietzsche's theory makes of tragedy a kind of
ballet or mime, combining the beauties of music and the plastic
arts but omitting poetry. It ignores our deep concern with what
men do as well as what they suffer, our sense that the figures of

[*31*]

tragedy, though 'larger than life', are truly human and do not think of themselves as 'beyond good and evil'. They are themselves torn and agonized by moral struggles and it is in their moral suffering that they often touch us most deeply. Schopenhauer and Nietzsche are alike in that in their attempt to express the essence of 'the tragic' they turn from poetry to music, and in Nietzsche's case to the visual arts also, as expressive of 'the tragic' in its purest form.

The Spanish philosopher, Unamuno, in a once-famous book, *The Tragic Sense of Life*, found the source of the tragic in the contradictions of man's nature. He thought that the root of the tragic vision of life lay in the hunger of man's heart for personal immortality which his noblest faculty, his reason, told him was a dream. Man knows himself to be immortal, because he cannot conceive of extinction, cannot imagine 'non-being'. Yet his reason tells him he must die, and he can find no rational defence against that rational knowledge. The tragic sense arises from the irreconcilability of the two kinds of knowledge, neither of which can be repudiated by man if he is to be true to his own nature. This is the root of tragedy; and here again it is seen to lie in a tension between two opposites: the presentation of two necessary but irreconcilable kinds of knowledge: that man knows himself to be above and outside nature and that man knows he is a part of nature. Kierkegaard also saw in 'contradiction' the essence of life, on which both the comic and the tragic are based; but the tragic, he wrote, 'is the suffering contradiction, the comical, the painless contradiction'. He thought that the difference between the tragic and the comic lay 'in the relationship between the contradiction and the controlling idea. The comic apprehension evokes the contradiction or makes it manifest by having in mind a way out, which is why the contradiction is painless. The tragic apprehension sees the contradiction and despairs of a way out.'[1] To both Unamuno and Kierkegaard the root of the tragic sense is metaphysical despair. Unamuno's analysis is moralized and theologized

[1] *Concluding Scientific Postscript*, trans. D. F. Swenson and W. Lowric (Princeton, 1941), 491.

by Reinhold Niebuhr.[1] Like all modern writers he takes death as
the great tragic fact: 'Man is mortal. That is his fate. Man pretends
not to be mortal. That is his sin. Man is a creature of time and
place, whose perspectives and insights are invariably conditioned
by his immediate circumstances.' But he

> ... builds towers of the spirit from which he may survey larger
> horizons than those of his class, race, and nation. This is a
> necessary human enterprise. Without it man could not come to
> his full estate. But it is also inevitable that these towers should
> be Towers of Babel, that they should pretend to reach higher
> than their real height; and should claim a finality which they
> cannot possess. . . . The higher the tower is built to escape the
> necessary limitations of the human imagination, the more
> certain it will be to defy necessary and inevitable limitations.
> Thus sin corrupts the highest as well as the lowest achievements
> of human life.

This Christian view holds an echo of such characteristic Greek
concepts as 'hubris', or overweening, and 'moira', a man's lot or
portion that he transgresses at his peril, though balancing against
these a necessity that drives man to attempt to transcend his limits.

This brief and necessarily inadequate running through of some
of the most influential theories on the nature of tragedy in the last
hundred and fifty years illustrates three things. There is a general
consensus that tragedy presents an image of life that enables us to
see into the truth of things. Philosophers and, in fact, any human
beings sufficiently reflective to have what may be called a 'philosophy of life', have found in tragedy support for, and illustrations
of, their own convictions and beliefs on 'Man, on Nature, and on
Human Life'. Secondly, as we would expect, these theories satisfy
fully only their creators. They all appear inadequate to others
when brought to the test of the interpretation of actual tragedies.
Either they fit only certain plays and are patently not applicable to
others, or they isolate in those plays one element, ignoring
elements which to some seem as significant, or even more so. And

[1] *Beyond Tragedy: Essays on the Christian Interpretation of History* (1938),
pp. 28–80.

it is noticeable that as the nineteenth century proceeds discussion of the essentially tragic moves further and further away from discussion of actual tragedies. Yet for all their contradictions, there is in the end a measure of agreement between all theories that are tolerable: they all discover in tragic art, or in the 'tragic vision', the co-existence of contraries, a union of opposites, whether in the emotions aroused, or in the concepts embodied.

I have left to last a formula that for me comes very near to expressing the nature of tragedy: the words that Beethoven scrawled, perhaps only in jest, above the opening bars of the last movement of his last quartet: 'Muss es sein?' 'Es muss sein.' He wrote above the whole movement the words 'Der schwer gefasste Entschluss' 'the Difficult Resolution'. The affirmation is in the same words as the question; only a hair's breadth, hardly more than an inflection of the voice separates them. Protest and acceptance are like expressions on the same face. According to their convictions and beliefs men attempt to conceptualize the protest and the affirmation; and according to temperament and even to mood the balance between question and answer quivers. Some find the essence of tragedy in the power with which the question cries out; others in the difficult final resolution. And ultimately, I think, we must accept that the way men read the image of life that a tragedy presents will depend on the bias of their temperaments.

In a very illuminating discussion of the problems of perception, Professor Gombrich[1] illustrated the different ways we can read a visual image by borrowing from the Gestalt psychologists an image that can be accurately described as a pattern of four linked equal rhomboids. We see it, however, at once, as a zigzagging band of four rectangles, like a strip of cardboard folded into four equal squares. But, so seeing it, there are two opposed ways of reading the image. We can see the band starting from behind, the two outer folds coming towards us and the central fold going away; or we can see it starting from in front, the two outer folds going away from us and the central one coming towards.

[1] *Art and Illusion* (1960), p. 220.

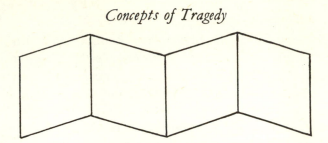

Whichever way we read it at first sight, with a little effort and some practice we can switch from one reading to the other; but we can never see both interpretations at once, nor can we ever see any intermediate possibilities. I do not know whether psychologists have discovered any correlation between the way the image is interpreted at first sight and the interpreter's psychological make-up, or if it is pure chance whether anyone at first sight reads it one way or the other. But this little problem where there is no 'right way' to read the image provides an analogy with the situation that arises when two fine critics such as Bradley and Granville Barker, while agreeing in their description of the course of events in *King Lear*, and of their connection in forming a design or pattern (as we may all agree that our image is made up of four linked rhomboids, that they all measure so much by so much, and the angles are so many degrees), yet read the image that Shakespeare presents in *King Lear* in opposed ways. C. S. Lewis provided an amusing analogy for the disagreements of critics over the 'meaning' of *Hamlet* by imagining a group of art critics looking at a picture. They agree that it is a very great work but are unable to agree 'what it is a picture of'. Most of them 'find something curious about the pose, and perhaps even the anatomy, of the central figure'. Various explanations are offered, until in a corner you find a knot of men whispering that the fact is that it is a bad picture, and the trouble with the central figure is that it is out of drawing.[1] But the analogy is a false one. The critics of *Hamlet* are not in disagreement over the subject-matter of the play and cannot be compared with persons unable to say whether

[1] 'Hamlet: The Prince or the Poem', British Academy Shakespeare Lecture, 1942, reprinted in *They asked for a Paper* (1962).

they are looking at a picture of 'The Raising of Lazarus', 'The Return of Bacchus from India', or 'The Death of Nelson'. They agree, in the main, on 'what happens' in *Hamlet*, the course of the action, the sequence of cause and effect: their dispute is as to how the action was meant to be regarded: to put it crudely, are we witnessing a story of defeat and failure, or a story of victory won at terrible cost, or, are both the concepts of defeat and victory irrelevant, and are we in fact watching the progressive revelation of the futility of all action in a world corroded by lust and dominated by the finality of death. As is well known, Eliot in a famous early essay took up the position of the 'knot of men whispering together' and declared that *Hamlet* 'is most certainly an artistic failure'. It was strange that a critic who protested so strongly all his life against the notion that great works of art can be 'interpreted' should have taken refuge in this solution of the problem presented by variety of 'meanings' that have been read into *Hamlet*. For it might well be argued that its supreme greatness lies in the differing interpretations it can sustain. As Professor Stuart Hampshire has written, it is 'the nature of the imagination that it generally deals in conflicts and contradictions, in dubious meanings, and not in definite conclusions and in unambiguous assertions. The energy in any imaginative work comes from that destruction of single-mindedness which allows different interpretations at different levels.'[1] But when Professor Hampshire goes on to say that 'the significance of any writer, whether poet or philosopher or historian, and that which makes him worthy of study now, commonly does not reside principally in the conscious intentions behind his work', I hesitate to agree. For if we say that 'significance' does not reside principally here, we are implying that it does reside principally somewhere else, and the notion of 'principally' I would question. Thus Beethoven described the slow movement that precedes his 'Difficult Resolution' as a 'süsser Ruhesang oder Friedengesang'—a sweet song of rest and peace; but Stravinsky writes: 'To me it is *Trauermusik*—not

---

[1] 'Commitment and Imagination', in *The Morality of Scholarship* (Cornell University Press, 1967).

necessarily a contradiction. The second variation is a dirge, in any case, and the prescience of death in the elegiac fourth variation is unmistakeable.'[1] The creative imagination has filled the intended song of consolation with grief and longing, the inconsolable seeking consolation. Yet one would hesitate to say that the artist's intention was not fulfilled and that the movement does not also marvellously console.

In tragic art, the imagination, the power that reveals itself as Coleridge declared in the balance and reconcilement of contraries, is seen at its greatest, since the elements it balances and reconciles are so sharply opposed and so harshly discordant. Most writers on tragedy stress the close as the source of tragedy's power to satisfy and console. But the pleasure, delight, satisfaction, consolation are surely felt throughout in the tension between the design and what the design strives to include, in the justice that is done to what baffles our understanding as well as to our understanding. Even at the close, in some form or other, there remain unanswerable questions. The design has to be strong. There must be a logic of events, not a mere sequence of distressing accidents, in order that the sense of ultimate mystery may be felt with its full power. Because we understand so much, we realize we understand so little. Although we are shown that this is how things are and how they must be, we are shown a universe that is not to the measure of men's minds or built in conformity to the desires of their hearts, that is ultimately inexplicable. Although it may be that

> *whether in Argos or England*
> *There are certain inflexible laws*
> *Unalterable, in the nature of music,*[2]

the rationale of those laws is not ours. Tragedy thus excites in Keats's words a 'momentous depth of speculation'. Its meaning does not lie principally either in the beliefs about the nature of things that it embodies or in the questions those beliefs arouse and do not satisfy but in their balance and interaction.

[1] Review of Joseph Kerman, *The Beethoven Quartets, The New York Review of Books*, 26 September 1968.   [2] *The Family Reunion*, II, i.

II

Tragedy in the Ancient World

A Shakespearian, who is not at home in either Greek or Hebrew
Literature, and who has to rely on translations, with occasional
reference to the original in Greek, and on the studies of classical
and Biblical scholars, cannot in discussing tragedy in the ancient
world do more than reflect on some of the striking differences and
likenesses that a student of modern tragedy is aware of when
turning to ancient tragedy. The contrast between Greek and
Shakespearian Tragedy has often been made by classical scholars
who, though deeply conversant with Greek thought and art, are
less at home in the world of Elizabethan England. Although my
handicap is a heavier one, I would all the same like to attempt
some comparisons from the other direction.

Greek Tragedy was religious, a sacred drama in more senses
than one. It was performed as part of the celebrations at the Spring
Festival of Dionysus. The priest of Dionysus occupied the seat of
honour and the altar of the god was at the centre of the orchestra
or dancing-floor. It took its subjects from the familiar heroic
legends of Greece, stories of heroes who were in many cases
objects of a cult. The stories were in themselves thrilling, exciting
and beautiful. They are among the great stories of the world and
have through the ages stimulated and challenged the imagination
of artists. They offered the chance to create great roles for actors
and gave occasion for lyric and philosophic reflection in great
choric odes. But other considerations appear to have dictated the
choice of these stories in the first place. They embodied religious
conceptions and exemplified the relation of men to the gods. This

is true even of those in which the gods do not take part in their own persons. This is a drama that is impregnated with the sense that powers beyond the wills of men operate in human life, in which it is possible for these powers to have an actual epiphany.

But having said that Greek Tragedy is religious in these senses, it is necessary to distinguish senses in which it is not. Although part of a religious festival and dedicated to the honour of the god Dionysus, the tragedies were not in themselves acts of worship. Though they may embody in their enactment of the legends the representation of ritual acts, and ritual prayers and invocations, they are not themselves to be described as a ritual. They are not the repetition of certain stereotyped acts designed to please or propitiate the gods. Performance and attendance at tragedies may be called a ritual, a liturgical act; but the tragedies themselves are representations of significant actions of the most varied kinds in which the powers of the gods can be seen, and from which men can learn wisdom by gaining understanding of the interaction of human and divine wills. Again, although the dramatist was limited in the choice of his subject-matter to:

Presenting Thebes or Pelops line
Or the tale of Troy divine,

and other traditional stories of gods and heroes, he was at liberty to find, in Aristotle's words, 'the right way of treating them'. The myths and legends were themselves fluid; they had not hardened into a received form nor had they been subjected to official interpretation. The dramatist could choose between different versions; he could suppress and supply. Although the main outline of the story was given and could hardly be changed, the disposition of events, the stress of the action, the motivation, the interplay between the persons and the gods, the particular role of the chorus and the nature of its comments were all open to the poet's choice.

In a certain sense, then, Greek tragedies are no more religious than any other plays. They were performed to an audience that watched, not for a congregation participating in a rite. Once the play had begun, the audience were not called on to participate in any other sense than the sense in which Henry James said we become 'participators by a fond attention' in what happens in a tragedy such as *Hamlet*. Some modern discussions of drama, contrasting modern secular drama in a commercially motivated theatre with Greek religious drama, speak almost as if the audience at a Greek tragedy enjoyed a communal religious experience comparable to taking part in the Holy Week processions in Seville, or attending a splendid and solemn Pontifical High Mass. But however moving the ceremonies, and however dramatic, and even theatrical, the spectacle and the music, there are moments in the procession, and in the Mass, when the mere spectator is made sharply aware that he is only a mere spectator. There are no moments in Greek drama that are comparable to the moment when the bell rings for the Elevation of the Host, and the auditors and spectators of what is being said and done are called to become worshippers. I cannot recall any moment in Greek drama that attempts, as Eliot did in *Murder in the Cathedral*, to convert an audience into a congregation, though even here it is a congregation listening to a sermon, not a congregation united in worship or prayer. And although this moment is effective with a special audience and in a special setting—in a chapterhouse, or a church, or in church ruins—it always seems slightly embarrassing and awkward in a theatre, demanding a different kind of participation from what drama may legitimately demand, or at least has demanded through the centuries. For perhaps one needs to say today that in Greek tragedies there is none of that confusion of audience and actors that is becoming a familiar experience in the modern theatre, when a neighbour in the stalls suddenly takes part in the play, or the auditorium is invaded by a shouting mob pouring up through the aisles, or the actors descend into it from the stage to secure the 'involvement' that is thought to be the most valuable theatrical experience. Whatever may have happened in the obscure beginnings of Greek Tragedy, the form of Greek theatres makes clear that the masterpieces of fifth-century tragedy were acted under conditions that set a great gulf between the actors and the audience. They sat there as spectators of a play, not as participators in a rite.

A much less questionable comparison than that between a Greek tragedy and a High Mass is the comparison between the tragedies of ancient Greece and the medieval mystery plays of Christian Europe, belated examples of which survive in remote rural areas of Eastern Europe, the Passion Play at Oberammergau being a sophisticated one. There are obvious resemblances here: the Craft Cycle plays, like the Greek tragedies, were performed annually at a religious festival, the Feast of Corpus Christi in the summer being as suitable for open-air performances as the Spring Festival of Dionysus was in Greece; and the Corpus Christi plays, like the tragedies, had liturgical origins. Many would go further and postulate a specially intimate relationship between authors, actors and audience on a basis of shared beliefs which is lacking in the modern theatre. They hanker after this as the ideal situation for drama as a great communal art, and see the audience at a Greek tragedy and the crowds around the pageants as united and spiritually involved in the representation of the beliefs by which they lived. While recognizing the crudity of the Corpus Christi plays when they are compared with the masterpieces of Greek tragic art, they believe that the secularization of English drama carried with it the seeds of dramatic decay, reducing to mere entertainment what should be the expression of what unites a culture: the complex of feelings and attitudes towards experience which makes up its religion.

An immense literature exists on Greek religion and Greek religious feeling and many famous and fascinating books have been written about it. But the more one reads, the more impossibly difficult it seems to become to imagine the mood, or surely one must say the various moods, in which the spectators assembled to watch a Greek tragedy. In thinking of past ages, we all tend to exaggerate their homogeneity. The effort of scholarship, particularly in the last fifty years, has been to break down our simple stereotypes. It has operated strongly in the field of Greek religion.

It now seems impossible to say how much even pious Greeks believed in common, and it is surely very unlikely that all the persons
who watched the drama were pious. The more one reads of Greek
religion the more striking its diversity appears, very ancient and
primitive conceptions and rituals co-existing with official religion,
with new cults of salvation, and with religious and philosophic
speculation. Fifty years ago we were taught to think in terms of
'stages' in Greek religion, primitive and barbarous conceptions
giving place to more refined. The Greeks were shown as pro-
gressing towards the 'morality touched with emotion', or the
thoughtful and reverent philosophic agnosticism which seemed to
many then to be the goal of humanity's spiritual progress. The
dominant conception of an evolutionary progress which operated
in all fields of human scholarship in the later nineteenth and earlier
twentieth centuries was at work here too. But it is now seen that
the concept of evolution is inapplicable to the short span of human
history, and our attitude to the primitive has changed radically.
We no longer regard primitive peoples and primitive art with
condescension, or confuse a simple social structure with crudity of
feeling, and lack of intellectual formulations with imaginative
immaturity. We study primitive societies with a new humility.
We find in them models which reveal to us the workings of the
human mind and the needs of man as a social being. And we find
in primitive art moving symbols that do not appear strange to us
if we explore what lies behind our conscious rationalizations of our
experience. This revolution in our attitude to the primitive has
affected our attitude to what were regarded as merely survivals as
superstitions of rituals and beliefs that had once had religious
significance. We have been taught to see in the culture in which
the great tragedies arose, as in other cultures, a complex of old and
new. Ancient rituals and ancient cults survived with new rituals
and new cults: ancient traditional wisdom co-existed with philosophic speculation. We ask ourselves how much of the numinous
and the awful the bright Homeric Olympians acquired when they
took over ancient chthonic shrines, and think of Socrates as not
jesting when he said he owed a cock to Aesculapius.

No doubt we also grossly exaggerate the homogeneity of the crowds in fourteenth-century Europe who watched the pageants which presented the great cyclic drama of Creation, Fall, Redemption and Final Judgment. Not all who watched can have been moved to a deeper apprehension of saving truths. But, impressive and moving as they are—and nobody who has seen the modern performances of the York Plays can question their beauty and power—there is a world of difference between these Biblical dramas and the tragedies of ancient Greece. Homer, it is often said, was the Bible of the Greeks. But the analogy holds in only a limited sense. Homer was a Bible in the sense that the *Iliad* and the *Odyssey* were the prime educational texts, the school-books of Greek culture. They were not sacred books in which a revelation, a *kerygma*, was enshrined. The Corpus Christi plays were far more than dramatizations of Biblical stories. Certain stories had to be included and are found in all the cycles. Others just as dramatic were not included. The test was whether the story had been interpreted as displaying the saving acts of God and pre-figuring the saving act of Christ. Both the choice of story and its interpretation were laid down. The freedom of the dramatist was severely limited. He could invent subsidiary episodes and develop minor characters; he was not free to discover or impose his own interpretation on either the parts or on the whole. The Corpus Christi plays are theological, illustrative of a coherent and comprehensive scheme of thought, a science of things divine. They are wholly untragic, not because the ultimate end of the whole cycle is happy but because they are unambiguous. The image they present can be read in only one way. They arouse no questions: they present answers. Theology, a fully articulated structure of thought, an intellectualization of religious experience and practice, can hardly be said to exist in classical Greece. When we discuss the religious significance of Greek Tragedy we are safe from that fatal confusion of religion with theology that bedevils the discussion of tragedy in Christian Europe.

It is difficult enough to enter imaginatively into anyone else's religious experience. When two thousand years and more of his-

tory separate us from authors and audience it seems rash indeed
to attempt to imagine oneself viewing a Greek tragedy in the
brilliant spring sunshine all those centuries ago. Responses that
seem natural and obvious today might not have occurred to me
then and elements I now overlook or regard as conventional
might then have aroused in me a religious response because they
echoed my own religious experience. We necessarily project into
the past our own concerns and our own way of seeing the world.
Our concepts of the past are historically conditioned. The com-
plexities and uncertainties of the world we live in have made the
picture of 'the Greeks' seem much less clear than it seemed in the
last century. Louis MacNeice, a classical scholar, at the time
teaching classics in Birmingham University, expressed flippantly
but seriously his sense of the difficulties he felt at being 'impresario
of the Ancient Greeks', mocking at the scholars of the generation
before his own:

> *the humanist in his room with Jacobean panels*
> *Chewing his pipe and looking on the lazy quad,*

who

> *Chops the Ancient World to turn a sermon*
> *To the greater glory of God,*

and adding:

> *But I can do nothing so useful or so simple;*
> *These dead are dead.*
> *And when I should remember the paragons of Hellas*
> *I think instead*
> *Of the crooks, the adventurers, the opportunists,*
> *The careless athletes and the fancy-boys,*
> *The hair-splitters, the pedants, the hard-boiled sceptics*
> *And the Agora and the noise*
> *Of the demagogues and the quacks; and the women pouring*
> *Libations over the graves*
> *And the trimmers at Delphi and the dummies at Sparta*
> *And lastly I think of the slaves.*

Tragedy in the Ancient World

And how one can imagine oneself among them
I do not know;
It was all so unimaginably different
And all so long ago.[1]

But MacNeice's Athens, which seemed in the thirties so much more plausible than Jowett's, is by now just as dated, too like Isherwood's Berlin to be convincing in the sixties. The audience has vanished and attempts to interpret the plays by their supposed reactions are more rather than less subjective than an approach that concentrates on the plays themselves, which have at least survived to endure our inquisition.

Ignoring the obvious differences of form, there are certain differences of temper, differences in where the tragic tension seems to exist which are striking when one turns from the tragedies of Shakespeare, and from modern discussions of tragedy influenced by Shakespeare, to a reading of Greek tragedies. Certain aspects of human existence which later ages have felt to be essentially tragic, and in which it has been suggested the roots of tragic art are to be looked for, do not appear to have seemed so to the Greeks, or at least are not emphasized in their tragedies. Man is shown as subject to natural necessity—the necessities of physical existence—as he must be in any drama that presents a truthful image of human life. But this basic fact of human existence: that we are at the mercy of our bodies, must grow old, lose our powers, and finally die, does not appear to have aroused in the Greeks that strength of feeling that makes so many modern writers speak of the fact of death as the prime tragic fact. For all their worship of beauty, the idealism of Greek plastic art, and their cult of the athlete, the burden of mortality, and of all that is included in the idea of mortality—the weakness of the changing body, the decay of our faculties, the final indignity of death and corruption, the empire of the worm—does not arouse a shudder, does not arrest the mind as being terrible:

Imperious Caesar dead and turned to clay,

[1] *Autumn Journal* (1939), ix.

Might stop a hole to keep the wind away.
O, that that earth which kept the world in awe
Should patch a wall t'expel the winter's flaw.

Hamlet's contrast between man's immortal longings and his mortality, his achievements and their dusty end, is everywhere in Elizabethan tragedy. It is not present in Greek. We find there an intense feeling for the dead, for the union of dead and living, the duties of the living to the dead, and the claims of the dead on the living, but not this horror at death itself. Tamburlaine's rage and grief at the death of Zenocrate, his repeated lament, 'And must I die and this unconquered', his final acceptance that 'Tamburlaine, the Scourge of God, must die', which he moralizes in his counsel to his son:

Nor bar thy mind that magnanimity
Which nobly must admit necessity,—

presents in the simplest form this idea of death as an outrage. Brachiano exclaiming:

On pain of death let no man name death to me:
It is a word infinitely terrible,

Claudio in his prison cell crying out:

Ay, but to die, and go we know not where;
To lie in cold obstruction, and to rot;
This sensible warm motion to become
A kneaded clod;

Hamlet soliloquizing on the 'dread of something after death' or brooding on the skull of the jester Yorick: these intense expressions of revulsion seem to justify Unamuno and Niebuhr in finding the root of tragedy in man's rejection and forced acceptance of the fact of death. But this seems to have little relevance to the roots of Greek tragic feeling. It is at first sight strange that this horror of death plays so large a part in Elizabethan tragedy, produced in Christian Europe, so that any English schoolchild, asked to distinguish tragedy and comedy, will at once say 'Tragedy ends

[*46*]

with death', as if death alone were enough to make a play tragic; or, at least, as if a play that did not end with death was not to be called a tragedy.[1] Aristotle did not think even an unhappy ending a necessity in tragedy, though he thought that the best kind of plot showed a change of fortune for the worse and was preferable to one that showed a change from misery to happiness. But misery to the Greeks did not necessarily mean death; nor do we find in Greek tragedy anything comparable with what seem to us quintessentially tragic summations:

> *And all our yesterdays have lighted fools*
> *The way to dusty death,*

or such an outcry as:

> *Thou'lt come no more*
> *Never, never, never, never, never.*

Such sayings come out of a different world of feeling from a world that gives us such sayings as 'Call no man happy till he dies; he is at best but fortunate' (Solon, quoted by Herodotus), or 'Not to be born is best' (Sophocles, *Oedipus Coloneus*). The chances and changes of mortal life, not mortality itself, the uncertainty of life, not the certainty of death, is recognized here.

Tragedy shows man as a social being, involved with his fellowmen, doing them good and evil, ordering his life and the lives of those around him, making mistakes according to his nature, pursuing his ends, sometimes selfishly, sometimes unselfishly, receiving good and evil at the hands of his fellows, acting wisely and unwisely in all relations of life as husband or father or wife or son or king or citizen. Greek tragedies are unashamedly didactic and deeply concerned with moral conduct. They tell us much of our moral duty and speak much of moral good and moral evil. Both characters and chorus express moral judgments and debate

[1] I imagine no French child would return such an answer, for the idea of death no more dominates French neo-classical tragedy than it does Greek, nor does it, any more than Greek, have necessarily to end with death.

moral issues. Milton made this the main ground for praise of the 'lofty grave Tragedians' when Satan advises Christ in *Paradise Regained* to learn

> *what the lofty grave Tragedians taught*
> *In* Chorus *or* Iambic, *teachers best*
> *Of moral prudence, with delight receiv'd*
> *In brief sententious precepts.*

The praise is put into the mouth of Satan, but Milton was man enough to give the devil his due and let him sometimes speak truth. Even the scornful Christ of *Paradise Regained* accepts this, and is willing to grant that by the light of Nature 'not in all quite lost', the Greek poets did express 'moral virtue'. These precepts arise as comments on a wide range of human conduct. But one kind of conduct that appears frequently in Elizabethan drama is not shown in Greek Tragedy. There exist characters of extraordinary beauty and heroic virtue, who are 'better than we are' in every sense. Greek Tragedy has its martyr heroine in Antigone who faces Cordelia across the centuries in uncompromising virtue, and some would add in stubbornness and pride in her virtue. What we do not find is monstrous and inexplicable wickedness, sheer malignity. The concept of villainy is at home in melodrama. Some would say it is alien to tragedy and quote Meredith:

> *In tragic life, God wot,*
> *No villain need be! Passions spin the plot:*
> *We are betrayed by what is false within.*[1]

It is true that no villain need be; but in Elizabethan tragedy villainy is rife:

> *Villainy, villainy, villainy!*
> *I think upon't: I think I smelt it: O villainy!*
> *I thought so then: I'll kill myself for grief:*
> *O villainy, villainy!*

Emilia's desperate cry expresses a horror at the idea of pure

[1] *Modern Love*, xliii.

wickedness, sheer ill-will. It is not only in sensational tragedies, verging on melodrama, that these monsters are found. In two of the very greatest of Shakespeare's tragedies we are presented with implacable malevolence, a hardness of heart that appals. There is no parallel among the figures of Greek Tragedy, or of neo-classic tragedy, for so terrible a figure as Iago, whose excess of motive makes clear his lack of any other motive but an evil will. Nor is there any parallel for the monstrous coldness of heart of Goneril and Regan. There is a mystery here that confounds the imagination and defeats explanation: *mysterium iniquitatis.* To Othello's cry:

> *Will you, I pray, demand that demi-devil*
> *Why he hath thus ensnar'd my soul and body?*

Iago simply replies:

> *Demand me nothing. What you know, you know.*
> *From this time forth I never will speak word.*

And there is no reply to Lear's agonized question: 'Let them anatomize Regan; see what breeds about her heart. Is there any cause in nature that make these hard hearts?' The thing is presented. We have to take it into our imaginations. This spiritual wickedness, this absolute ill-will, cannot be reduced or explained. Fearful and criminal actions are the very stuff of Greek tragic plots; but they are performed in error or in madness, or in a passion that overwhelms the bounds of reason and moral restraint. It might be said that no great Elizabethan tragedy contains such a frightful deed as Medea's slaughter of her children; but Medea has suffered intolerable wrongs, compared with which Iago's resentment at being passed over, even if we take this as a serious grievance, is a ludicrously inadequate motive; and Goneril and Regan have been loaded with benefits. It is the cold rationality, the deliberate and stony-hearted decision to inflict pain that terrifies in Iago and Lear's cruel daughters. It terrifies because it is inexplicable; we cannot get behind it or explain it. It is something against which we cannot arm ourselves.

When Milton's Satan praised the Greek tragedians for the delight their brief sententious precepts gave, he saw this moral teaching as subordinate to their main concern, which was to treat:

Of fate, and chance, and change in human life:

Fate—the doom that man cannot escape, *Chance*, the accident which no foresight can prepare against or prudent wisdom evade, *Change*, the law of life, of all things living in time, those reversals by which from prosperity a man is suddenly cast down, or from honour brought to dishonour. Satan, in thus describing the vision of the course of things in the tragedians, no doubt deliberately omitted, in his advice to the Christ to learn moral wisdom from the tragic poets, the presence and operation in the tragedies of Powers whose operations to some degree control, and whose presence makes in some degree comprehensible, the vicissitudes of human life. But the severe Christ does not forget them, and in scorn he contrasts the Greek poets who:

> *loudest sing*
> *The vices of thir Deities, and thir own*
> *In Fable, Hymn, or Song, so personating*
> *Thir Gods ridiculous, and themselves past shame,*

with the poets of Sion in whose songs:

> *God is prais'd aright and Godlike men,*
> *The Holiest of Holies, and his Saints.*

These Powers among whom deity is diffused, the gods and goddesses, the demi-gods, the heroes who have become demi-gods and are in some way numinous, are a part of the universe. They are within, not outside, the whole scheme of things. The Olympians might be flippantly characterized as the upper classes of the universe, displaying the disrespect for ordinary morality and the sexual laxity usually associated with an idle aristocracy, along with a strong consciousness of their superiority to the common run of mortals and resentment at attempts to usurp upon their privileges. The gods are immortal and free from care. They are supernatural—not subject, that is to say, to natural necessities and to the laws that govern physical life. They express both men's sense that they inhabit a universe which they do not understand, and their attempts to understand it. They can be thought of in different ways, as expressing different aspects of forces felt in human life. They reveal themselves in forces in the natural world which are outside man's control and which disturb the regularities of nature —storms that wreck his ships, winds that drive him off his course, lightnings that blast, the thunderbolt. Or their power can be felt in impulses in human nature that appear to master us from without, psychic forces that drive men to do things that seem against their nature, or more terribly in the onslaught of madness. Or they may by their intervention reveal laws that govern human life, which operate obscurely to our limited understanding but shine out when the gods act, necessities which man must acknowledge and which, if he neglects to recognize them, will destroy him; sanctions on human conduct are in the power of the gods. When we feel 'it was not I that did it', or feel ourselves 'driven' to speak or act in a way that seems foreign to our nature, so that we say 'I can't think what I was thinking of to do it', the gods are working: if not the divinities, at least the daemons. Eros or Aphrodite takes away a man's judgment and power to choose. We recognize this when we speak of 'falling in love': we have not chosen to be thus obsessed. This personal experience is universalized when we see 'Vénus toute entière a sa proie attachée', and recognize in Phaedra the victim of the power of a terrible goddess. Invasions of rage can take possession of a man, or madness descend upon him and drive him to enormities, or he may become inspired by a power from without by which he sees as the gods see, and as men may not, the inevitable future. The gods intervene in human affairs. At times they appear simply hostile to man, 'jealous and interfering' as Herodotus calls them; not evil or malignant but concerned to keep man in his place. Too much happiness or too great success, or too great an achievement calls out a supernatural response, to reduce man to the sense of his human lot. He must be humbled, brought down, taught wisdom and self-knowledge.

This feeling is moralized into the doctrine of the punishment that awaits 'hubris', which sees man as rightly punished for arrogance, for forgetting he is a mortal and acting as if he were a god, and by this usurpation on divine prerogative failing to honour the gods. Unmixed happiness is not for man, is not his lot or portion, his 'moira'. If he forgets this, disaster will swiftly remind him of it. But besides this 'jealousy' of the gods against men, which humbles the proud, they have also a concern that wrong should not go unpunished and that evil acts should bring evil doom. Their instruments here are the wills and passions of men, and disasters such as plague and famine, and the ancient powers that avenge the spilling of blood and embody the notion of blood-guilt, the Furies. There is a complex of conceptions here that appear conflicting; for what has arbitrariness to do with law and jealousy with justice? Such contradictions always appear when the attempt is made to formulate religious beliefs. The effort of theology is to find an intellectual solution for these contradictions, and to harmonize into coherence man's various and conflicting apprehensions of the divine, his knowledge of what is not fully knowable and can only be known in aspects. But such efforts to create systems of belief come long after the creation of the great tragedies.

In them there is the basic contradiction, that all is the work of the gods and all is the work of men. Professor Dodds has used the phrase 'overdetermination' or 'double determination' to express this picture of a universe where the gods work in and through men. Some actions are 'doubly determined', acts of men that are willed by the gods. Professor Kitto prefers to speak of action on a dual plane. The events have their own human, natural and psychological necessity, so that they would 'make sense' if the gods were not there; but their meaning is shown by the presence of the gods, since the gods see laws and understand causes, and thus bring about ends that they know must be, whereas man brings about ends that he does not foresee. Modern scholarship has moved rather away from the older conceptions of Aeschylus the theologian, Sophocles who 'saw life steadily and saw it whole', and Euripides the rationalist, exposing the follies and immoralities of religion. It finds in the tragedies less thought and more imagination, less theology and more religion.

In discussing religious conceptions it is difficult to rid oneself of Christian ways of thought and even if one avoids specifically Christian terms not to give a Christian colouring to the words one employs. The rationalist is not in much better case here than the Christian, since he too inherits the legacy of the Christian centuries and his conception of religion is inevitably affected by Christian thinking and practice. Terms such as sin and repentance come more naturally to us than pollution and purification. It is difficult for us to accept and enter into the omnipresent ancient conception of pollution as an objective reality, without importing into it the Christian idea of wilful sin and deliberate transgression of divine commands. It is very strange to us to think of a man as incurring guilt and becoming a polluted object as a consequence of deeds done, without respect to his motive in doing them, or even to whether he was conscious of the nature of his acts. And stranger still to think of such pollution as spreading like an infectious or contagious disease. We have reduced the Greek word 'miasma' to a mere poisonous exhalation, a natural physical phenomenon, as we have restricted pollution to material pollution, something that happens to water supplies or food. The stress on motive is everywhere in modern drama; but the notion on which Yeats built his religious drama of *Countess Cathleen*—

> *The Light of Lights*
> *Looks only on the motive not the deed,*
> *The Shadow of Shadows on the deed alone*—

is utterly un-Greek. If in the *Oresteia* we find this concept of pollution, along with the concept of ancient and inherited guilt, profoundly moralized; and, after the long sequence of crimes breeding fresh crimes as their punishment, glimpse in the acquittal of Orestes, the cleanser of his house, some recognition by the powers above of the upright heart and pure, no such sense of a divine Justice lightens the story of Oedipus, where the presence of the gods is felt in the oracle of Apollo which must be fulfilled.

Without diminishing the strength of Oedipus's character, his rashness and over-bearing temper and the fearful irony by which he himself uncovers the secret of his birth, nothing can rationalize the awful necessity by which he incurs the pollution that from him infects all Thebes, the pollution inseparable from incest and parricide. This pollution his self-blinding and acceptance of the role of outcast makes visible, and it is his acceptance that he is polluted that gives him grandeur.

Like the concept of pollution, the concept of oracle in Greek religion and Greek religious thought cuts Greek Tragedy off from the tragedy of Christian Europe. Shakespeare uses oracle in *The Winter's Tale*, a romance or tragi-comedy. But in his tragedies, as Bradley rightly said, it is difficult to discern the idea of Fate, with which the conception of oracle is so closely linked. In what many would regard as his greatest tragedy, *King Lear*, the word Fate does not even occur; and the absence of the true religious sense of oracle is apparent if we look at *Macbeth*, the nearest Shakespeare came to writing a classical tragedy. With its lack of a sub-plot, its concentration on two main characters, its opening messenger speech, its murder taking place off-stage, and its patent Senecan echoes, *Macbeth* would seem to be an attempt by Shakespeare to write in a stricter form to suit an ancient theme. For *Macbeth* is oracular in the sense that the action is dominated by an unfolding future which hangs over it, and like the ancient oracles the weird sisters' prophesies are equivocal and 'keep the word of promise' to the ear while they break it to their hearer's hope. But the riddling prophecies of the three hags who meet with Macbeth and Banquo have no religious sanction behind them. They cannot be compared with oracles delivered at the greatest of all Greek holy places, the shrine of Apollo at Delphi. To any audience, as to Banquo, the weird sisters are 'instruments of darkness', and the heart of the play does not lie in Macbeth's fulfilment of their prophecies. He is not doomed to kill his king in ignorance. He is tempted to make certain of what is promised. *Macbeth* is not a tragedy of Fate, but of crime and punishment. It is a tragedy of the will and of the terrible attraction of evil. It uncovers a mystery in its simple pattern of sin and retribution, but it is not the mystery of a destiny that cannot be avoided and that man will the more surely bring about the more he attempts to avoid it.

The gods in Greek Tragedy are much concerned with what men do. They care and yet they do not care. When they take on a moral colour, it is a negative one. They are swift to punish. They are, to quote Milton's Eve, 'great Forbidders'. Even Socrates, when speaking of his *daemon*, said that it told him what *not* to do: the voice of conscience barring the way, not impelling. But beyond their roles as rebukers of human pretensions and 'heavenly justicers', the gods have, in Professor Dodds's phrase, a 'formidable holiness'. They are other than men. The depth of Greek religious feeling is most felt in this sense of the divine otherness: the inhumanity of the gods, whose ways are not as our ways and who cannot share human pain. This sense of awe at the gods as not accountable to men, can be felt at the close of *The Women of Trachis*, when Hyllus speaks of the cruelty or iniquity of the gods and the chorus can only reply that 'all that has happened is of Zeus'. Or it is felt at the close of the *Hippolytus*, where Artemis, although she speaks loving words to her mangled votarist Hippolytus, leaves him when he enters on his death agony, since the gods may not look on death. Pre-eminently the mystery and the terror of the divine is felt in the graceful and smiling stranger of the *Bacchae*.

In modern discussions of tragedy it is often assumed that the prime tragic question is the question raised by undeserved suffering, and many today would say that it is this that raises an unanswerable 'why' and makes it a mockery to claim that the scheme of things has any justice. Justice cannot mean only retribution and never reward, and gods who do not care for their own, or cannot help them in their need, have ways that cannot be justified. Aristotle was content to say that the spectacle of a very good man passing from happiness to misery would be too painful to contemplate on the stage. Otherwise he does not touch on what is called 'the problem of pain'. It is not a problem that the tragic choruses much revolve. As a recent editor of the *Poetics* observes,

Aristotle knows no powers that can be questioned as to why the world is as it is. His philosophic god is 'inside the process, eternally actualising potentiality. Events happen in the way they must in the light of what has happened before and of human decisions superimposed on the logic of events'.[1] And for the tragedians, the gods who acted in the world and in some sense ruled it, had not made it. As the fact of death seems to many today the prime tragic fact of experience, so the fact of undeserved, and still more of innocent suffering, of the enormous injustice with which calamity strikes, seems to many today the great tragic question. But this question arises out of a different religious tradition.

What separates the religion of the Hebrews, and those religions which spring from Judaism, Christianity and Mohammedanism, from all other religions is not merely the doctrine of the unity of God, but the assertion, with which the Bible opens, that in the beginning God created the heaven and the earth. This tremendous leap of the religious imagination seems to have occurred some time in the sixth century B.C. It transformed Yahweh, the god of the salvation of Israel, who visited and redeemed his people and led them out of the Egyptian bondage, the God of Exodus, into the Creator of the universe without whom nothing was made that was made. There are creation myths in other religions, and concepts of supreme Beings in other cultures; but this assertion of the dependence of the whole universe and of everything that happens within it on the will of a Being that is without it and beyond it is the strange thing. Because it is so familiar we do not realize how strange it is. As Professor North has written in his commentary on *The Second Isaiah*:

> Most readers of the Bible take the doctrine of creation for granted, without pausing to reflect how singular, unique, and indeed, well-nigh incredible a doctrine it is. Nowhere except in a few psalms is it extolled as part of the *kerygma*—if the word may be used of the Old Testament recital of Yahweh's 'Saving Deeds'—and yet without it there would be no kerygma. That is why the first verse in the Bible begins with it, likewise the

[1] D. W. Lucas, *Poetics* (1968), p. 120.

[56]

first clause in the Creeds. Outside the Bible it has no parallel, except in the Qur'an, which is Judaism and Christianity at second hand. The concept of creation is not obvious, nor does it come naturally to mankind. Everywhere except in the Bible, interpretation of the universe is naturalistic, and worship is, in one form or another, worship of 'the great god Pan'. This is true of the religion of classical Greece, of polymorphic Hinduism, of humanism in its various forms, of the current concept of 'one single branching metabolizing protoplasm', and of the popular idea of 'the life force' as the creative agent in the universe. Outside biblical theism all interpretations of the universe are so many more or less refined forms of what the Old Testament stigmatizes as the worship of Baal, Baal being conceived as the personification of the life process. Once man is left to his unaided reason for an explanation of the universe, he invariably seeks to explain it *from the inside*, and the resultant philosophy or religion—call it what we will—is some form of naturalism, and worship is worship of 'the creative process' rather than of God the Creator of the process.[1]

Professor North is writing as a Christian and a theologian who accepts the doctrine of Creation as the cornerstone of revelation. In my present context I am content to regard it as simply a tremendous leap of the human imagination. Bacon declared he could not imagine this mighty universe had come into being without a mind behind it: the vast majority of the human race seems to have found no difficulty in imagining so. Bishop Gore once said that the most difficult text in the Bible was the text 'God is Love'. It is only difficult if by God we mean the Creator of all that is. It is not at all difficult to believe it if we only mean that the highest and best thing in the world we know is Love: that 'Love is God'. This raises no problems, for we are simply divinizing the highest moral value we have found in our experience.

The Hebrew doctrine of creation, like all profound religious conceptions, creates problems and raises new mysteries. It would seem that it raised at once and presented to the Hebrew consciousness the existence of undeserved suffering as the prime mystery of human existence. It seems so to many who discuss tragedy today

[1] C. R. North, *The Second Isaiah* (1964), p. 14.

because they have inherited, even if they may have rejected, this Hebrew sense of the ubiquity of the divine will throughout the universe, and of the consequent responsibility of God, if there is a God, for all that happens in it. Hebrew literature gives us two great works, not tragedies since they are not works of art designed to please, nor written for performance, but very close to tragedy in their feeling for the mysterious and awful aspects of human life: the Book of Job and the Suffering Servant Songs of Second Isaiah.

Milton spoke of the Book of Job as a 'brief epic' and took it for a justification of the form of his *Paradise Regained*. Like *Paradise Regained* it has little narrative content, and apart from the pro- logue and the brief epilogue is wholly given over to the speeches of Job, the speeches of the comforters, and the final speech of the Lord out of the whirlwind. Though not dramatic it is thus quasi- dramatic in form, a dramatic debate resolved by an epiphany, and is unique in Hebrew literature. The prologue is mythological, with the Lord allowing Satan to torment and afflict the exception- ally righteous Job, to test whether his piety is merely the result of his prosperity and whether, if he is sufficiently tormented, he will 'curse God'. This celestial or, as one might prefer to call it, infernal bet between the Almighty and Satan is never referred to again and forms no part of the main debate. The brief epilogue in which everything is given back to Job and more, twice as much as he had before, like the prologue, seems irrelevant to the great central poem. It used to be argued that both the prologue and the epilogue were later additions; but I think this view has now been aban- doned. Their presence may be justified on literary grounds. The author must of necessity at the beginning beg the whole question of whence and why misfortune falls on Job, for it is its inexplic- ability that is the core of the argument; and at the close he has no other way to vindicate Job's integrity and confound the counsel- lors but to show him, in spite of his intransigence, 'favoured by God' in the only way they can recognize. The Book of Job is a work of literature, not a philosophical or theological treatise. It has to have a beginning and an end. Its grandeur lies in the

author's resolute refusal to accept an explanation of the problem
presented by the sufferings of the righteous. Against his friends
and against the brash young man Elihu, Job stubbornly refuses to
accept that his sufferings can in any way be regarded as just treatment of him. To all the attempts of the comforters and of Elihu
to vindicate the justice of God, he replies by justifying himself. He
is 'righteous in his own eyes'. It is this that kindles the anger of
Elihu, a clever young man who knows all the answers and who
comes nearest to being a professional theologian. But the Hebrew
writer does not accept, as a Calvinist might, to use Pauline words,
that all human righteousness is 'filthy rags'. The answer that Job
receives is of quite another kind. As has often been said, it is,
intellectually, no answer at all. It turns on the assertion in magnificent language of the very belief that raises the question: that God
is the Creator of the whole marvellous and strange universe we
find ourselves in. It is patently irrelevant to the question of the
justice of God's dealing with men to say 'Look at the hippo-
potamus and the crocodile'. But what other answer can there be?
If God's governance of the universe seems to conflict with our
own highest notions of what is just and right, are we to abandon
our notions of what is just and right, or are we to abandon belief
in his governance? This insoluble intellectual dilemma is presented
in the Book of Job in all its insolubility with beauty and power, as
it presents itself to the religious consciousness. God is righteous,
but his ways are not our ways. We cannot 'confine the intermin-
able nor tie him to his own prescript'. But we must maintain our
ways before him. What convinces Job is not argument, but an
overwhelming sense of the majesty and reality of God: 'I have
heard of thee by the hearing of the ear: but now mine eye seeth
thee. Wherefore I abhor myself, and repent in dust and ashes.'
Yeats's father, J. B. Yeats, discussing tragic catharsis and the
cleansing of the passions in tragedy, wrote, in a letter to J. B.
Quinn:

> I omitted the best illustration of all—the Hebraic conception of
> Jehovah: He is the image of Terror—terror itself—but so over-
> whelmingly magnificent that the beauty of the conception

cleanses away all the pain, and as the energy of the terror inspired so is the intensity of the feeling of Beauty. Prostrating
themselves in abject submission, these Jews were and are pene-
trated through and through with the delirium of Beauty. It is
that which inspires the psalmists.[1]

There is much else in the psalmists' conception of the Lord beside
a 'terrible beauty'; but it is this that inspired the poet who wrote
the Book of Job.

The Book of Job rejects any attempt to explain human suffering
in terms of the guilt or sin of the sufferer. It does so in quasi-
dramatic form, and so it is not wholly improper to set it beside
Greek Tragedy as a work of literary art. The Suffering Servant
Songs of Second Isaiah are a very different matter. They are
prophecy and neither narrative nor dramatic in form. Problems of
interpretation are extremely difficult here: whether the Servant is
the afflicted people of Israel, or the perfect type of a Servant of
God, or a prefiguration of the Messiah, as the writers of the New
Testament took him to be and as they represented Christ as regarding him. The whole mode of Hebrew prophecy is so different
from the mode of artistic creation, of fictional presentation, that
it seems improper to discuss these profound and mysterious
assertions as we discuss an image of life presented in an action
that is complete, having beginning, middle and end. But if the
tragic sense of life in Christian Europe is to be discussed, this most
profound reversal of the almost universal ancient belief that suffering is a mark of divine displeasure cannot be disregarded. The
Suffering Servant Songs assert that there is, as all religions have
felt, a connection between human sin and human suffering: they
deny that the calculus is one that we would make. And going
further, they exceed the Book of Job's rejection of suffering as
punishment and see the Sufferer as Chosen. Shakespearian tragedy
appears in a world in which it is possible for Bacon to write, without seeming paradoxical, 'Prosperity is the blessing of the Old
Testament; Adversity is the blessing of the New; which carrieth the
greater benediction, and the clearer revelation of God's favour'.

[1] B. L. Reid, *The Man from New York* (1968), pp. 365–6.

III

Shakespearian Tragedy

The conditions in which Shakespearian Tragedy appeared were wholly different from the conditions of Greek Tragedy. The Elizabethan theatres existed on sufferance, the players being under the protection of great nobles or the court. They were a perpetual object of suspicion to the more bigoted and vociferous among the godly and to the civic authorities. The plays they performed had to be 'allowed', to see that there was 'no offence' in them, that they did but 'poison in jest', and that they did not touch on weighty matters of state or on religion. The stories the Elizabethan dramatists worked on came from any and every conceivable source, ancient or modern, except one. They were not bound to any corpus of traditional material and could dramatize any tale that struck their fancy. But, with very rare exceptions, such as Peele's *David and Bethsabe*, they left the Bible alone. The theatre lived on popular support; it gave the people what they wanted. Players and playwrights had to please to live. The Elizabethan theatre was a commercial enterprise. It was as true of it as of the modern theatre that:

> *The drama's laws the drama's patrons give,*
> *For [they] who live to please must please to live.*

But in pleasing their patrons, the playwrights had to make sure that they did not displease the authorities. The failure to use for dramatic purposes such a splendid storehouse of dramatic stories as the Bible is explicable on all grounds. The Bible was sacred, not to be thought of as literature and treated as a mere source book among other collections of narratives. It had received authoritative interpretation. The stories of Old Testament heroes and kings could not be manipulated by the dramatist's imagination, or filled out, as other stories were, with invented incidents and lively subplots. Such rudimentary expansions as are made in the Corpus Christi plays, in Mak the wicked shepherd, Cain's idle and impudent servant, and the shrewish Mrs Noah, conflict with the Protestant reverence for Scripture. But even if it had been possible to treat Biblical material with the same freedom as the dramatists showed in their handling of history and legend, in a period of acute religious controversy explicitly religious stories and themes were far too dangerous to be treated in a public theatre. There was a powerful movement among the pious and learned, both Catholic and Protestant, in the sixteenth century to create a Divine Drama, as well as a Divine Poetry.[1] Its monuments, whether in English or Latin, are dramatically still-born. A belated result of all these endeavours, and the only one of any literary merit, is *Samson Agonistes*, which Milton said was 'never intended for the stage'.

The secularity of Elizabethan drama is obvious. It cannot in any possible sense be called a sacred drama. But a secular drama is not necessarily irreligious. It may still expound religious ideas and express religious attitudes and feelings. Both writers and audience had a concept of what a tragedy was or ought to be, and of what kind of story a tragedy unfolded. They were both heirs to a long tradition by which such stories had been moralized and given a religious interpretation. When a tragedy was presented on the stage, the audience came with certain expectations. They expected to see a story with a calamitous ending, a change of fortune from happiness to misery; and they expected the end to be the death of the main character at the very least, and probably the deaths of many others. The stage would be hung with black. They also expected a tragedy to be historical. If it did not deal with well-known figures and famous stories from world history that were familiar

[1] For an account, see Lily B. Campbell, *Divine Poetry and Divine Drama in Sixteenth-century England* (University of California Press, 1959).

to all, it should at least present what gave the illusion of being historically true. When Hamlet exclaims ' 'A poisons him i' th' garden for his estate. His name's Gonzago. The story is extant and written in very choice Italian. You shall see anon how the murderer gets the love of Gonzago's wife', he is commending the play as not being a fiction, something its author has made up. The notion that tragedy is historical goes back to a famous fourth-century contrast between tragedy and comedy which declares, among other things, that all comedy invents its plots but that tragedy often relies on history.[1] There are very few tragedies in the Elizabethan period of which one cannot say 'The story is extant'. When the Elizabethan dramatist turned to tragedy, like the Greeks, he took a story to dramatize, to give shape to, to find a meaning in. On the rare occasions when a plot was invented, or when we do not know of a source—the most famous being Kyd's *Spanish Tragedy*—the dramatist made every effort to give his play historic actuality, so that it would at least seem as if it had really happened.

Although it would be wrong to limit the medieval conception of the tragic to stories of the Falls of Princes, this is the dominant conception in medieval definitions of tragedy. Tragedy, it is declared again and again, displays the power of Fortune in overthrowing and bringing to misery the great and prosperous: 'What other thing bewailen the cryings of tragedies but only the dedes of Fortune that with an unwar strok overturneth realmes of gret noblee', as Chaucer renders Boethius. Or again 'Tragedye is to seyn a ditee of prosperitye for a tyme that endeth in wretchedness.' Tragedy showed a change of fortune from good to bad—its ending was unrelievedly catastrophic. It was a story of Kings and Princes and it was 'historical', not made up. The tragic writer looked in history for examples of Fortune overthrowing Kings and Kingdoms. No logic in the course of events was necessary for tragic effect. No cause need be hinted at except the inherent in-

---

[1] 'Omnis comoedia de fictis est argumentis, tragoedia saepe de historia fide petitur' (Evanthius, *Treatise of Tragedy and Comedy* included in many Renaissance editions of Terence).

stability of all earthly things. The lesson of tragedy is that nothing abides and that change is the law of life. But it is random change. This simple and sorrowful idea of the uncertainty of all earthly happiness—yesterday a king, today a beggar—is capable of considerable artistic elaboration. It can sustain a religious interpretation—that here we have no abiding city—and direct us, as Chaucer does at the end of the tragedy of *Troilus*, to set our hearts on heaven; and it can enforce a moral, rebuking human pride and demanding compassion for the unfortunate, since as they are today we may be tomorrow. It holds within it also a tragic terror as well as a tragic pity: the sense of awe that the spectacle of blind Belisarius begging for an obol inspires. It can also arrive at a tragic ambiguity if developed with imaginative power. As Professor Farnham has shown,[1] in order to evoke to the full the contrast between the height of noon and the darkness of night, to give the 'unwar strok' of Fortune its full force, the pomps and vanities of this world must be shown as truly pompous and glorious. In affirming the instability of all earthly glory and the weakness of all human greatness, the imagination finds itself affirming glory and greatness.

In the later Middle Ages a different conception of the lesson of history conflicts with this concept of Fortune's irrational power: that the calamities that destroy men are self-wrought, that we bring what is wrongly called misfortune on ourselves. Boccaccio, in his *De Casibus*, is far more concerned with man's responsibility than with Fortune's fickleness. The huge sixteenth-century collection of narrative verse-tragedies modelled on the *De Casibus*, *The Mirror for Magistrates*, the first edition of which appeared in 1559, accepts this view whole-heartedly. The *Mirror* is a glass for kings and rulers, to warn them of the tragic consequences of sin. History is seen here as the field of God's judgments, a concept set forth at great length and in majestic prose by Ralegh in the preface to his *History of the World*. History repeats itself; but its repetitions are not meaningless. They spring from the invariable laws of God by

---

[1] See Willard Farnham, *The Medieval Heritage of Elizabethan Tragedy* (University of California Press, 1936).

which sin brings calamity. This is the Tudor concept of the lesson of history, and the view that tragedy, which draws its matter from history, exists to display the just judgments of God is the most common view of tragedy in the Elizabethan period. It is often very crudely expressed, as in *The Revenger's Tragedy*, whose recipe for tragic excellence is 'When the bad bleeds, then is the tragedy good'. But even a writer we think of as sophisticated, John Donne, preaching after 1620, with the great age of English tragedy behind him, reveals in an aside in a sermon that this is what he would expect to see if he went to a tragedy. He asks his auditors how they would reply, 'If I should aske thee at a Tragedy, where thou shouldest see him that had drawne blood, lie weltring, and surrounded in his own blood, Is there a God now?'.[1] Tragedy, in this conception, displays the world as rational, as *The Theatre of God's Judgments*, the title of a book of tragical stories. Particularly it displays *God's Revenge for Murder*, the title of another collection, from which Middleton took the plot of *The Changeling*. Sidney puts first, when commending 'high and excellent Tragedy' that it 'openeth the greatest wounds, and sheweth forth the Ulcers that are covered with Tissue' and 'maketh Kinges feare to be Tyrants, and Tyrants manifest their tirannicall humors'. But interestingly and significantly he adds the contrary concept that Tragedy 'with sturring the affects of admiration and commiseration teacheth the uncertainty of this world, and upon how weake foundations guilded roofes are builded'.[2] Tragedy thus, as Sidney sees it, shews both the certainty of judgment and the uncertainty of all mortal things.

There was a third strand in the Elizabethan inheritance: the conception of tragedy derived from reading the tragedies of Seneca. Formally Seneca had little or no influence on the popular theatre; but his tragedies offered to the Elizabethans a different conception of tragedy from the conception that it displays the

[1] *Sermons*, edited by G. R. Potter and Evelyn M. Simpson (University of California Press, 1953-62), viii, p. 332.

[2] *An Apology for Poetry*, in *Elizabethan Critical Essays*, edited by G. Gregory Smith (1904), i, p. 177.

power of Fortune or the just judgments of God. Much darker conceptions are embodied in Seneca's lurid dramas. There is first the notion that tragedy is primarily concerned with the monstrous and outrageous, with 'to deinon', acts that appal the imagination. It seems probable that the Elizabethan theatre with its roots in popular taste would have been sensational even if Seneca's plays had been unknown; but Seneca gave precedent and authority to dramatists aiming at high tragedy to explore the terrible. As a concomitant of this conception of the tragic action as centred in a deed of horror, there goes an emphasis on the inner workings of minds torn and driven by passion, and these are analysed in speeches of considerable rhetorical elaboration. The destructive forces in human nature are present in Seneca's tragedies as they are not in the tragedy of Fortune or the tragedy of Judgment. Beyond this, there is felt in them the presence of the supernatural, or rather the praeternatural, operating in human affairs. Christianity had been born into a world deeply conscious of the existence of demonic powers, haunted by the fear of 'spiritual wickedness in high places'; but by the end of the Middle Ages Christian supernaturalism had become unambiguous and unmysterious. Angels and devils were inhabitants of a rational and ordered cosmos in which they, like everything else, had their place. When Marlowe puts his Good and Bad Angel on either side of the stage in *Dr. Faustus*, they arouse in us no real sense of the supernatural. They address the reason and the conscience, not the imagination. They belong to the world of the morality play and the pageant, which instruct us by making vivid what is not to be questioned and exist to confirm rather than to trouble our beliefs. On a stage committed as the Elizabethan stage was to tragedy as the representation of an image of historical reality, the sense of the supernatural or the praeternatural pressing upon human lives could not find expression in the presentation of gods and goddesses and furies intervening in human affairs. It finds expression in the ghosts of Elizabethan drama, which have the ethical ambiguity of human beings with the addition of a non-humanity that makes them terrifying, in a fascination with madness and with the dark underworld of magic and witchcraft, and in the presentation of inexplicable wickedness and malice. These are things that:

shake our disposition
With thoughts beyond the reaches of our souls.

Here, as elsewhere, what is crude and often unimpressive in other dramatists is raised by Shakespeare to heights of expressiveness. He transformed the 'filthy, whining ghost' crying 'Revenge' into the majestic, troubling, and questionable figure of Hamlet's father's ghost; no other dramatist has equalled him in presenting the awful visitation of madness, or in suggesting the degrading horror of witchcraft, or the destructiveness of malice. All these are things that bring into question man's understanding of the universe he moves and acts in.

I should like to suggest two things. The secularity of the Elizabethan drama, the fact that the dramatists were not committed to the exposition of sacred doctrines, allowed the tragic writer something of the same liberty of imagination in rendering his apprehension of the nature of things as the absence of a formal theology gave to the Greeks. The terms and concepts used, the intellectual framework within which they wrote and the religious and ethical formulations which the dramatists shared with their audience, by which they shaped their plots and out of which they provided sententious comments on human conduct and human affairs, were the terms and concepts familiar to their age, fundamentally Christian, hammered out during sixteen centuries of Christian thought. These *idées reçues*, making up the 'Elizabethan World Picture', have been much discussed and examined in this century. Such examination is profitable, indeed essential to our understanding, as long as we do not regard these ideas as alone providing us with the 'meaning' of the tragedies. They provide affirmations out of which questions arise, in the interplay between which the richness and inexhaustibility of the 'meaning' lies. The questions are as much Christian as the affirmations, in that they are aroused by the affirmations.

[67]

Further, the conspicuous weakness of the Elizabethans in criticism, particularly in the criticism of the drama, the conflicting conceptions of what tragedy was, the variety of dramatic forms and dramatic conventions available as models when Shakespeare began to write, gave him almost complete freedom as an artist to follow where his creative imagination led him. The stage he wrote for was as free from the pressures of critical orthodoxy as it was free from the pressures of theological orthodoxy. He was no more under the necessity of writing critical prefaces to justify his procedures than were the Greek tragedians. Shakespeare was a working actor and professional dramatist who made a lot of money by his profession. He was an artist engaged not in systematic but in imaginative thinking, with an imagination that was fundamentally dramatic. Phrases and images throughout his work show how naturally he thought of life as itself a kind of play in which men and women shape their roles and their way of addressing their world and their fellows. His imagination continuously exercised itself in the creation of different and new images of life, exploiting and enlarging by his exploitation the potentialities of the Elizabethan stage. He was a ceaseless experimenter, the opposite of the successful writer who goes on turning out competent 'repeats' once he has found what he can do and what will please. He continually turns to different models, transforming them as his imagination works on them. The initial stimulus seems sometimes to have been the challenge of an occasion: the request to write a play for a wedding, or the need to provide a play that would particularly appeal to King James. He had also to meet the challenge of writing for a repertory company of which he was a member, giving his fellows parts they could play and opportunities for their particular talents. We perhaps owe to a boy actor who happened to have a beautiful singing voice the moving snatches of song he gave to the distracted Ophelia and the heart-rending beauty of Desdemona's Willow Song. Perhaps his voice had cracked when Shakespeare wrote *King Lear*, and Cordelia's beautiful silence, her extreme unloquaciousness, which is so impressive in a play in which everyone else talks so much and so loudly, was something that Shakespeare's imagination 'found' in writing for a company in which the best boy actor could only speak in a voice that was 'soft, gentle and low'. Certain painters are remarkable for their special feeling for paint, as are certain composers for their special feeling for the orchestra, or for the piano, or for the human voice. Shakespeare the poet has the same kind of special feeling for the theatre, for the actor's art and for that most objective of all literary forms, the drama. His instinctive need to experiment is nowhere more apparent than in his tragedies: in the diversity of material he turned to for tragic plots, in the completeness and distinctiveness of the worlds of the different tragedies, in the extreme differences in their designs, or their dramatic lay-out, and in their highly individual and characteristic poetic styles. He was at the height of his powers and his popularity when he turned to the great sequence of tragedies which begins with *Julius Caesar*, and virtually created our modern concept of what tragedy is. He created by the force of his imagination and the adventurousness of his art what, if the term were not liable to be misunderstood, might be called 'Christian Tragedy'. But since this term has implications that I should wish to avoid, it might be better to say he created 'Gothic Tragedy', enjoying the same freedom to develop the form as the Greek dramatists enjoyed in creating Classical Tragedy.

'The problem of belief is probably insoluble', as Eliot once wrote. How much men really believe of what they say they believe is not measurable. The relation of a writer's personal beliefs, whether by this we mean the formulas to which he gave assent or the convictions by which he lived, to his works is as problematical and as delicate a matter as the relation of his biography to his works. There are certain statements we can make about Shakespeare and religion. One is biographical and least important. Still, it is just worth making. Whatever truth there may or may not be in the tradition that he 'died a Papist', he was never, as far as we know, in trouble with the authorities over recusancy. He must have conformed and attended church regularly. This might mean indifference and a desire to avoid trouble and the paying of fines, or it might not. The other facts are facts that we gather from his written works. First, he knew the Bible extremely well, much better it appears, to judge by the amount of Biblical reference and quotation in the plays, than the majority of contemporary dramatists. But the fact that the language of the Bible comes so readily and easily to his mind may only reveal his superior literary sensitiveness, something no more and no less significant than his response to the pregnant expression of popular wisdom in proverbs. He appears, all the same, to have been a Bible reader and not merely a hearer. It was established many years ago that he knew the Bible in the Geneva version: that is in the version which men read in their homes, not in the version appointed to be read in churches.[1] Then, more recently, a theologian has examined the explicitly theological references in the plays, and has declared that Shakespeare had an informed knowledge of current theology: that when he refers, whether seriously or in jest, to a theological conception, he gets it right. He was, in Professor Frye's words, 'theologically literate'.[2] This is not surprising. The range of Shakespeare's informed understanding in so many and so varied fields of human activity is one of the most striking features of his plays. It has led to a great deal of biographical speculation, the theories neatly cancelling each other out, for he could hardly have found time in the 'missing years' to follow all the occupations about which he is said to show professional knowledge. His informed knowledge of the law has made some postulate a training as a lawyer's clerk, and is, of course, one of the arguments by which the Baconians buttress their fantasies; his expert seamanship has made others send him voyaging, while his military knowledge has made others suggest he trailed a pike in the Low Countries. Others send him travelling, perhaps with a company of players, in northern Italy which he seems to know more of than could be got from books. We take his expert, practical knowledge of husbandry, of field sports, and of country ways for granted in a Warwickshire boy. But a great many of his contemporaries had a

[1] See Richmond Noble, *Shakespeare's Biblical Knowledge* (1935).
[2] See Roland Mushat Frye, *Shakespeare and Christian Doctrine* (1963).

country boyhood and do not show such practical understanding and such a fascination with the actualities of rural life and rural sports. We need not therefore suppose that Shakespeare's theological expertise implies any particular theological training or even any deep theological concern. It is only another example of his power to 'get it right' in sphere after sphere, of his immensely alert intelligence, and his lively response to all forms of human activity. It would be astonishing if, living in an age dominated by theological controversy, Shakespeare had not been 'theologically literate'; just as, living in a greatly litigious age, he was 'legally literate'. So this again does not take us very far, except that, as Professor Frye justly observes, it should make us careful not to attempt to read theological ideas into Shakespeare's plays unless we too are 'theologically literate'. There has been in this century a notable body of criticism that has attempted to make many of the plays illustrative of theological conceptions, almost allegories of the Christian scheme of redemption. Against the basic assumptions of such readings, of an audience alert to the existence of such hidden senses and expecting to find them everywhere, Professor Frye establishes that the theological authorities most revered in Elizabethan England wholly accepted the integrity and independence of literature as a mirror of human life, and as a vehicle of moral truth, and did not look in it for illustrations of the truths of revealed religion. His demonstration of this, and his exposure of the naiveté of some of the theological interpretations we have been treated to, make his book a valuable cooling card.

I would like to add a third fact from the plays. There are to be found in them, and again this does not seem to me to be so true of the other Elizabethan dramatists, most beautiful and impressive expressions of distinctively Christian conceptions. Obvious examples are Isabella's plea to Angelo to show mercy as he must hope to find mercy himself, and the serious understanding of what penitence demands in King Claudius's soliloquy. Beautiful and impressive expression is, of course, given to many other ideas; but no other dramatist shows, I think, such imaginative response to the quintessentially Christian concept of forgiveness, or gives

[*71*]

such memorable expression to it. But again one must add that one cannot argue from this. Shakespeare is our greatest poet of human nature, and all we can say is that if his play requires that a character should speak as a Christian he enters imaginatively into Christian experience and feeling with characteristic understanding and sympathy.

These facts are only mentioned in passing for I am not concerned to attempt to answer the unanswerable question of Shakespeare's personal piety or impiety. And when I call Shakespearian Tragedy 'Christian Tragedy' I do not mean that I think of it as expounding analogically or otherwise the Christian scheme of Redemption, or as in any way concerned, in Milton's words, with 'praising God aright and Godlike men, the Holiest of Holies and his Saints'. I mean that the mysteries it exposes are mysteries that arise out of Christian conceptions and out of Christian formulations, and that some of its most characteristic features are related to Christian religious feeling and Christian apprehensions; and that the particular differences I have tried to suggest between Greek and Shakespearian Tragedy arise out of the revolution in religious thought that the foundation of the Christian Church brought about. The Christian doctrine of God destroyed the concept of oracle, so important in Greek religious thought and so widely present in Greek plays. The Christian God may be a *Deus Absconditus*, but if he speaks to man it cannot be 'in words deceiving'; and the related concept of Fate cannot co-exist with the doctrine of Providence, however obscure and devious to human eyes the ways of Providence may appear. The Biblical doctrine of creation and of God's rule over history has made the problem of the existence of evil and the inequity of reward and punishment on earth seem the prime question that tragedy raises, so that many in discussing a tragedy find it necessary to regard it as either obscurely justifying the divine economy, or impugning it as immoral, or denying its existence. Again, although at first sight it seems strange that in Christian Europe, whose prime doctrine was the Resurrection, the mere thought of death and physical corruption was almost enough in itself to arouse tragic feeling, and most discussions of tragedy today assume its end should be death and regard death as the great tragic fact, it is surely this very doctrine that marks or creates a different attitude to death. The doctrine of the Resurrection, which is very different from belief in the survival or immortality of the soul, makes death more than the payment of our debt to nature, or the release of the soul from imprisonment in the body. The moment of death becomes the moment of judgment, and the moment when man, through the victory of Christ over sin and death, is remade. If creation is the cardinal Hebrew doctrine, the Resurrection, or the new creation, is the cardinal Christian doctrine, on which all else hinges. It concentrates the imagination on the absoluteness and finality of death, as the great test of faith. No other religious tradition has stressed as the Christian tradition has the duty of contemplating death and preparing for death. In the later Middle Ages it comes to obsess the religious imagination. As Art becomes less and less symbolic, less and less concerned to present in images the mysteries of faith and more and more concerned with the presentation of observed reality, death is presented by great artists in all its physical reality, with a sense of the overwhelming pathos of the dying or dead body, and in all the gruesome actuality of corruption on tombs. It was strange that Lord Clark in his lectures on 'Civilisation' took Hamlet's 'Let her paint an inch thick, to this favour she must come' as an expression of Renaissance melancholy and scepticism. This moral had been preached for centuries; and for well over a hundred years before Shakespeare made Hamlet moralize among the graves, it had been given striking visual expression in the contrast between the richly clad lady lying on the tomb and the horrifying figure of the *transi* below. One can see why in a drama committed to the presentation of historic reality, of the true course of things in this world, after centuries of Christian experience, one finds a sense of the terror and mystery of death as one does not find it in classical tragedy.

A related feature of Shakespearian Tragedy is the dominance of the hero whose death is felt to be essential to the tragic resolution.

While many and varied strands of thought and feeling, and many and varied conceptions of human nobility have contributed to the creation of these great figures, I would like to suggest that the modern assumption, largely based on Shakespeare's tragedies, that tragedy displays the fate or fortune, the deeds and sufferings, of an exceptional individual whose experience is the central experience of the tragedy, is not simply a consequence of Renaissance individualism but has its roots farther back. The pattern of a single life, ending with death, underlay all Christian thought and speculation and provided an increasing focus for devotion and the imagination throughout the later Middle Ages. No other religious tradition builds into its confession of faith the narrative of a life lived from the cradle to the grave at an actual period of history, and finds in this a revelation. We are accustomed to take for granted the emergence in post-classical times of the notion that tragedy is essentially narrative. With the death of a living theatrical tradition the notion of tragedy as the 'imitation of an action' becomes the notion of tragedy as 'a certain story', and a story of *'him* who stood in great prosperity', the life-story of an individual. From the presentation of crisis it becomes the presentation of process. It is surely an interesting change. I cannot think it is unconnected with the Biblical stress on history as meaningful, on the fact that the sacred books of Christianity contain so much historical narrative and so many life-stories. The Christian conception of history as providential includes the notion of the providential ordering of individual lives in a pattern that is only completed at the moment of death. The Christian stress on the individual, on the importance of all his actions and words as under judgment, on individual accountability—'of every idle word you shall give account'—and on his worth in the sight of God—'The very hairs on your head are numbered'—makes the whole life-experience of man revelatory, so that the meaning of life is seen in a curve, an unfolding of a single destiny, not in a knot that is untied. Process and time are an essential element in Shakespeare's tragedies: the element of story is very great. This can hardly be because he was unaware of the dramatic value of concentration, for in comedy he more than once preserved the unities. In his first comedy, *The Comedy of Errors*, as in his last, *The Tempest*, the action is the untying of a knot. He preserves the unity of place in many others and comes very near to unity of time. In his tragedies he never attempts it. The nearest he comes is in *Othello*, of which Johnson said 'Had the scene opened in Cyprus . . . there had been little wanting to a drama of the most exact and scrupulous regularity'. But *Othello* does not open in Cyprus. Its splendid first act is set in Venice, which gives to *Othello*, above all the other tragedies, the design of the old tragedy of fortune. The whole first act shows Othello at the height of his fortunes, the saviour of the Venetian Republic and the chosen husband of Desdemona. It is true that this design combines with another design, for Othello is not the victim of Fortune's whim; but the compression of events in Cyprus, which Johnson rightly, I think, saw as an attempt by Shakespeare to attempt the concentration of classical tragedy, is only achieved by playing the tricks with time on which so much ink has been spilt. Even that great classicist Jonson, in his two Roman tragedies, followed history and showed the course and not merely the climax of his story. There is an irreducible narrative element in all Elizabethan tragedies, and pre-eminently in Shakespearian, as if the serious representation of reality involved the presentation of man as living in and through time and its meaning was to be understood through the developing experience of an individual.

Like all tragedies, Shakespeare's tragedies are impregnated with moral values and moral feeling. But they have a distinct ethical flavour when compared with classical tragedies and, I would add, with neo-classical. Johnson, as some have thought very oddly, thought it a great merit of Shakespeare that, whereas in other dramatists the 'universal agent is love', Shakespeare had a truer sense of the nature of human life. 'Love', Johnson declared, 'is only one of many passions, and as it has no great influence upon the sum of life, it has little operation in the dramas of a poet, who caught his ideas from the living world, and exhibited only what he saw before him.' It seems an odd comment on the author of

Othello and *Antony and Cleopatra*, not to mention the author of the so-called 'happy comedies' and the problem plays. But, if we restrict love to passionate love, sexual love, Johnson's comment is not untrue when we look at Shakespeare's tragedies. They are very little concerned with what is elsewhere a great tragic theme, the struggle of reason against passion. Love as a kind of madness, a guilty passion, is not at the centre of any Shakespearian tragedy. Even in *Antony and Cleopatra* the two main characters are singularly free from any sense of guilt. But Shakespeare's tragedies are pervasively concerned with love in a much wider sense: love of parents for children, and children for parents, of friend for friend, and husband for wife, of master for servant, and servant for master. This is the source of the greatest suffering in them: Hamlet's grief at his father's death and horror at his mother's falseness, Othello's agony at his loss of faith in his wife, Macbeth's discovery that he has condemned himself to a solitude in which all men hate him, Lear's discovery that his own flesh and blood reject him. The destruction, by breaking or poisoning, of the ties of affection, the bonds that bind man to man in the giving and receiving of love, is peculiarly central to Shakespearian tragedy which also contains glimpses of a spiritual happiness that has the quality of blessedness and peace in the exchanges of love. The supreme example is the meeting of Lear and Cordelia when like a loving and dutiful daughter she kneels to ask his blessing and he struggles to kneel to her for her forgiveness. These were gestures Shakespeare's imagination accepted as right from the old play of *King Leir*. But Lear's vision of their life together in prison is all Shakespeare's own. This state is pictured for a moment in Hamlet's cry to his mother, 'And when you are desirous to be blest, I'll blessing beg of you.' In the painful, dark, mistrustful world of *Hamlet*, one short scene stands out, an oasis of light, the exchange of love of Hamlet and Horatio, where Hamlet gives voice to his heartfelt love and admiration for his friend's selfless steadiness, his trustworthiness. In *Othello*, the reunion of Desdemona and Othello in Cyprus conveys a sense of pure and absolute happiness, of a love that is 'peace not rage', that I do not think can be paralleled in

[76]

any other tragic writer. There wells up again and again in Shakespeare's tragedies the sense of the beauty of 'mercy, pity, peace and love' as the true 'human image'. It is not deliberate and laboured but expresses itself naturally and instinctively in moments and in short phrases. It overwhelms us in the beauty of Desdemona's dying lie, strikes us in passing when Cassio, who has 'a daily beauty in his life', hearing Othello reply 'Ay' to the question 'Did you and he consent to Cassio's death' exclaims 'Dear general, I never gave you cause', and at the close pays tribute to the man who had tried to have him murdered: 'For he was great of heart.' It touches us when Brutus notices his page is tired and sleepy, or when Lear in his enormous anguish sees that the Fool is shivering. The villains in Shakespeare are those who seem wholly to lack this fellow-feeling. They neither have the capacity to love nor feel the need of love. They are themselves alone, living by a perverted reason by which they coldly see other men as existing to serve their envious egotism and desire for power. Shakespeare twice altered the motive his source provided for a villain. In the sources both of *Much Ado About Nothing* and of *Othello*, the slanderer was actuated by the desire to be revenged on a woman who had refused his love; slighted love had turned to hate. But neither Shakespeare's sulky Don John, a mere sketch of the envious man, nor his terrible Iago is conceived as capable of loving. Being incapable of love they are incapable of pity. Shakespeare's earliest attempt to write a tragedy, *Titus Andronicus*, a farrago of sensational crimes and brutalities, has a plentiful crop of villains. It also makes repeated use of one dramatic gesture, kneeling. Its most recent editor owns to being completely baffled by the amount of kneeling in the first act, and finds it difficult to suggest by the stage directions who at any moment are supposed to be on their knees and who have got up. It is a clumsy use of a symbolic gesture by an inexperienced dramatist. Its implications are clear as the play proceeds and the gesture recurs. The play is about suppliants disregarded, pleading unanswered, pardon not given, forgiveness refused. At the close the body of Tamora is flung out to beasts and birds of prey with the comment:

Her life was beast-like and devoid of pity.

Shakespeare accepts as do all the writers of his age the stock conception of reason as the image of God in man and the possession
of reason as what differentiates man from beast. But what differentiates man from man in Shakespeare's universe is not superior
rationality but capacity to feel love and grief, be touched by
fellow-feeling, to be moved to pity, and to show mercy. He was
called the 'gentle Shakespeare' by his contemporaries. It is not an
adjective we should expect to be used of a great writer of tragedies,
plays full of violence and cruelty. But there is in the tragedies an
ideal of 'humanity' which the word 'gentle' fits. Shakespeare was
much aware of the Stoic concept of human nobility and the Stoic
ideal of the wise man who 'rules the stars'; but the essentially self-
regarding ideal of *apatheia* has not entered at all deeply into his
imagination of the human ideal. Donne's beautiful sermon on the
text 'Jesus wept'[1] is far more consonant with the moral colour of
Shakespearian tragedy than any Stoic pronouncements:

> Inordinatenesse of affections may sometimes make some men
> like some beasts; but indolencie, absence, emptinesse, privation
> of affections, makes any man at all times, like stones, like
> dirt. . . . When God shall come to that last Act in the glorifying
> of Man, when he promises, *to wipe all teares from his eyes*, what
> shall God have to doe with that eye that never wept.

Shakespeare had a sufficient historic sense to be aware of Roman
ideals of conduct and in his Roman plays there is a kind of conscious high-mindedness that marks off Romans as almost a special
species of *genus humanum*. But though Antony in his tribute to
Brutus praises his disinterested virtue, Brutus himself in death
does not find comfort in the thought of his own rectitude but in
the fact that his friends have been true to him. And when Richard
II wishes to disclaim his royalty and declare that he is a man like
other men, his last proof of his common humanity, beyond the
fact that like all men he tastes grief, is that he needs friends. In a
masterly paragraph on Shakespeare's sonnets, C. S. Lewis de-

---

[1] *Sermons*, ed. cit., vol. iv, No. 13.

clared that 'However the thing began—in perversion, in convention, even (who knows?) in fiction—Shakespeare . . . ends by simply expressing love, the quintessence of all loves, whether erotic, parental, filial, amicable, or feudal', saying of the sonnets as a whole, with their two loves of comfort and despair, that they are an expanded version of Blake's 'The Clod and the Pebble', and that in his celebration of 'The Clod' Shakespeare opens a new world of love-poetry 'which has hardly a precedent in profane literature'. He concludes: 'In certain senses of the word "love" Shakespeare is not so much our best as our only love-poet'.[1] Lewis is thinking of the transformation in the word *Amor* or *Love* by the inclusion in it of all the senses that are not included in the word *Eros*. Love in these senses plays little part in neo-classical tragedy. It is everywhere in Shakespearian tragedy both in its presence and in pain and horror at its absence.

In general then I find in the characteristically unclassical range of time in Shakespearian tragedy, and in its focusing on the experience, a developing experience, of a single individual, formal elements that have a correspondence with Christian concepts, and see the form that Shakespeare developed as growing naturally out of and expressing a way of regarding the world of human experience created by the Christian centuries; and I find in the ethical temper of Shakespearian tragedy, with its emphasis on pity as the great human virtue, and in the images he so constantly presents of love as a giving, not an asking, a distinctively Christian conception of human goodness. These images appear often in unexpected places and incidentally: not merely in the selfless dedication of Desdemona or in the role that Cordelia plays throughout *King Lear*, in Kent's self-forgetful fidelity, or Horatio's undemanding affection, but in, for instance, some fleeting words of the fiendish Lady Macbeth who knows

> *how tender 'tis*
> *To love the babe that milks me,*

as in her husband's famous image of Pity as a naked new-born

---

[1] *English Literature in the Sixteenth Century* (1954), pp. 504–5.

babe. In these senses then I think of Shakespearian tragedy as 'Christian' when contrasted with classical tragedy and with tragedies modelled on or attempting to rival ancient tragedy. But going beyond these generalities, I find also a relation between the tragic balance of protest and acceptance in Shakespearian tragedy and mysteries that particularly oppress a Christian consciousness in the dialectic between faith and experience.

In a very obvious sense both *Hamlet* and *Macbeth* are Christian tragedies. Both are set in a Christian world and when the characters employ religious language it is Christian language that they use. In *Hamlet* Shakespeare very remarkably set an originally barbarous story of revenge for blood in the world of his own day and not in an ancient world in which men did not know that the Lord had said 'Vengeance is mine, I will repay'. *Hamlet* is remarkable for the amount of Biblical quotation and reference it contains, and at more than one point the action turns on a theological point: doubt over the nature of apparitions of the dead besets Hamlet, or, as some would say, provides him with an excuse for delay; and his refusal to kill the King at prayers, when he appears to be in a state of grace, and Claudius's 'hardening' of heart and inability to repent is the turning point of the play. There is a constant preoccupation with how men and women meet the moment of death; the importance of a good or a bad end comes up again and again. Almost nobody in the play makes a 'good end': the unhappy Ophelia's is left doubtful, the elder Hamlet, Polonius, Rosencrantz and Guildenstern, Gertrude and Claudius all have 'no shriving time allowed', and are taken in their sins. The exceptions are the two young men on whom the burden of wrongs done by others falls: Hamlet and Laertes. They have time to 'exchange forgiveness', and die pardoning each other for the wrongs each has done the other. The text just quoted 'Vengeance is mine' is never cited. Kyd uses it in a perfunctory way in *The Spanish Tragedy*, where Hieronymo sets it against the Senecan injunction 'Strike and strike home'. But Shakespeare never raises this question. He was not writing a problem play on the ethics of revenge, to provoke an audience to thought on what is proper conduct by contrasting one mode of action with another. Nor was he writing an exemplary play to teach us our Christian duty. Tourneur attempted this in *The Atheist's Tragedy*, where the hero, on good supernatural advice, waits in patience, leaving 'revenge unto the King of Kings', who obligingly provides it. In *Hamlet* we are in a world of moral dilemma where the burden of setting things right torments the conscience and cannot be shrugged off and left to the powers above.

Yet the presence of a power above acting in and through men is strikingly felt in the design. It is a design that becomes apparent as the play proceeds and is only clear at the close. Everything that seems chance and accident, and the play as it proceeds is full of the apparently random and accidental, is seen at the end to have contributed to the fulfilment of the ghost's command, and ironically almost every action has brought consequences the opposite of what the doer purposed. Most ironically of all, Hamlet's delay, with which he reproaches himself so bitterly, is a main element in bringing about the hoisting of Claudius with his own petard, that self-destruction of the wicked who fall into the pits they have digged for others, which is so characteristic a feature of the denouement of an Elizabethan Revenge Play.[1] The satisfaction of the close is real, in that everything has been exposed, and all appear in their true colours. The situation at the beginning is intolerably false: the royal bed of Denmark is a couch for luxury and damned incest, the King is a treacherous fratricide, masquerading as a genial and lawful monarch, his main prop and stay is an unreverend old man armed with the shabby wisdom of the world. At the close, the ulcer has been cut out, the boil has swelled, burst and discharged its poison, the smell in the drains has been located and they have been flushed out. Any metaphor used has to be a filthy one, because *Hamlet* is about the exposure of 'something rotten'. Many recent studies make it unnecessary to enlarge on Hamlet's role as 'scourge and minister', the surgeon who explores

[1] For an extended discussion, see my *The Business of Criticism* (1959),

the diseased body, by so doing provokes 'further evil', and finally in death cuts out the 'canker of our nature'. It is Hamlet himself who sees himself as 'scourge and minister', speaks of 'a divinity that shapes our ends', uses the specifically theological term 'special Providence' and from the beginning shows awareness of 'more things in heaven and earth than are dreamt of in your philosophy'. 'Over-determination', or 'double determination', is strongly present in the ironic design of *Hamlet*: its presence is acknowledged by the hero, as by others: 'Our thoughts are ours, their ends none of our own.'[1]

But if we say that the design of *Hamlet* reveals the working of a law that turns the devices of the wicked against themselves, brings hidden deeds of darkness to the light of day, and unkennels all occulted guilts, and speak of *Hamlet* as a tragedy of divine justice, however much we qualify the assertion by acknowledging that the operation of this law is cruelly indifferent to the fates of those destroyed in its slow working-out, we have left out what else this design reveals. We have traced a line but ignored what the line bounds. We have turned *Hamlet* into a play of action, which it is; but we have ignored the fact that it is also a play in which action seems irrelevant, and 'what happens in *Hamlet*' is not what *Hamlet* is about. We have omitted all those intolerable dilemmas of the conscience that the chief actor among those who unwittingly fulfil the design suffers; and the discovery as the play proceeds of the omnipresence of evil. This world, which at its first appearance, except for the menacing appearance of the ghost, is so ordinary, almost domestic, and easy-going on the surface, is riddled with treachery and false faith, and rotten with corruption. Evil is discovered by Hamlet in himself as well as in others as the play proceeds, in words and acts that 'unkennel the occulted guilt' in him. Even more there grows throughout the play a sense of horror at man's entanglement in the flesh, at the indecencies of physical existence: that we begin in 'the rank sweat of an enseamèd

---

[1] For an extended discussion of *Hamlet* as a religious tragedy, and comparisons of *Hamlet* with Greek tragedy, see H. D. F. Kitto, *Form and Meaning in Drama* (1956), pp. 246–337.

bed' and that we end as food for worms. There is no devil in
Hamlet. Claudius is not a fiend; his motives are all too human. He
has lusted after his brother's wife and wanted his brother's crown;
having obtained both he will stop at nothing to keep what he has
got. And, of the two motives, we have no doubt which is the
stronger. No tragedy in the world gives such depth of meaning to
all that is meant by the world, and even more by the flesh, as the
enemies of the spirit of man and of his peace, or more calls in
question our human condition, 'crawling between earth and
heaven'. Hamlet's immense world-weariness, which alternates
with his disgust, echoes the Calvinist Fulke Greville's lament at
the 'wearisome condition of humanity':

> *Born under one Law, to another bound:*
> *Vainly begot, and yet forbidden vanity;*
> *Created sick, commanded to be sound.*

Hamlet's sickness of soul, or what has been called his 'terrible
morbidity', led Eliot to speak of him as 'dominated by an emotion...in *excess* of the facts as they appear'. It is true if we take the
facts as merely the murder of his father and the adultery of his
mother. His horror at carnality goes far beyond revulsion at his
mother's infidelity. Like his brooding on death, which equally at
once repels and fascinates him, it springs out of a world of thought
and feeling quite alien to the world in which Orestes fulfilled the
duty of avenging his father. As Christianity transformed man's imagination of death, it also transformed his attitude to his animal
nature, his sexuality. Hamlet may be called 'morbid' in his disgust
at the 'nasty sty'; the same charge has been brought against many
Christian writers from St. Paul onwards. Among religions
Christianity is remarkable for the severity with which it regards
'the flesh' and the sins of the flesh, finding that there is a law in a
man's members that wars against the law of his mind.

Within a design that declares that history is not meaningless
Hamlet conducts an inquisition into the very conditions of our
existence as historic beings, exposing all that conflicts with any
sense that there is a providential ordering of human affairs, pre-

senting the world as a kind of maze in which no right way for-
ward appears. The duty laid on Hamlet is qualified by an impossible condition: 'Taint not thy mind'. But how can man, in a
corrupted world, set the world right without using the world's
weapons and acquiring the world's stain? 'History', as Acton
observed, 'is not a web woven by innocent hands.' How find a
right way in a world where nothing can be done 'with perfect
conscience', and even more how can a 'bare bodkin' cure a world
infected by 'rank corruption mining all within'? The disease is
beyond the remedy's power and yet it cries out for surgery.
Orestes's fearful choice was between two duties, two pieties: his
choice brings on him pollution. Between Orestes and Hamlet
there lie centuries in which the concept of sin, of personal responsibility, of purity of motive as the test of virtue have made for
agonized searchings of conscience. *Hamlet* is a Christian tragedy
in the sense that it is a tragedy of the imperatives and torments of
the conscience. It shows human history as the field of God's
judgments, while showing too that:

> *History has many cunning passages, contrived corridors*
> *And issues, deceives with whispering ambitions,*
> *Guides us by vanities. . . .*
> *Neither fear nor courage saves us. Unnatural vices*
> *Are fathered by our heroism. Virtues*
> *Are forced upon us by our impudent crimes.*
> *These tears are shaken from the wrath-bearing tree.*[1]

The design of *Macbeth* is far simpler and more obvious than the
design of *Hamlet*. Macbeth gets precisely what he knew he would
get from the murder of Duncan and does not get what he hoped,
in spite of his knowledge, that he would get. He has judgment
here: he never gets the reality of kingship, 'solely sovereign sway
and masterdom'. There could hardly be a simpler tragic pattern
than *Macbeth* presents and no sub-plot· distracts us from the
spectacle of the inevitability of retribution. Some crimes are so
frightful that they arouse the world against their perpetrator,

[1] T. S. Eliot, *Gerontion.*

making of 'safety' a mirage that lures the criminal to fresh crime, while the desired goal, 'to be safely thus', recedes ever further and further. The moral design of *Macbeth* could not be clearer: it is given almost allegorical significance when his fear-ridden court is contrasted with the holy English court. Yet no tragedy is more full of dark questions, of a sense of almost panic terror—there is 'riding by night' on the air and on the earth—and it revolves profound and unanswerable metaphysical problems. They are not stated or argued: they are none the less there. What is it that lures men against their judgment and against their better nature to do what revolts them? Why do they persist in a course that leads them, as they know it will, to destruction? Why does a prophecy of future greatness arouse in one man a mild response, and in another not a vision of greatness but a vision of murder? To say that Macbeth is driven by ambition explains nothing. It is a word one can use of a young man working hard for an examination or an industrious apprentice: it does not explain murder. The mystery of the perverted will, the attraction of the dreadful, and the imagination of all that is meant by damnation are far more powerfully presented in *Macbeth* than in the explicitly metaphysical and theological tragedy of *Dr. Faustus*. This is what it means to become one of the lost, to be forever outside the fold in the hell of solitude and of despair. The nature of the will and the extent of its freedom was the grand point at issue in the debate of the Reformation. Why do those who know both good and evil say 'Evil be thou my good' and trample on their conscience? Why does Macbeth go to murder Duncan, as Bradley said, like a man who has nerved himself to perform a terrible duty? Macbeth is not driven by passion or madness, the great sources of criminal acts in ancient tragedy, and Shakespeare has been careful to remove all the possible excuses for the murder of Duncan which were present in the stories he used in Holinshed. He makes the deed as black and monstrous as possible; and Macbeth's 'supernatural solicitings' are horrible and fear-inspiring. No devil disguised as an angel of light tricks him. The witches are loathsome figures and the bloody dagger a thing of horror. But no bright vision comes to the help of his struggling conscience. He is led into temptation and not delivered from evil. The play of crime and retribution reveals not only its rigid logic of cause and consequence but also something for which we cannot find an adequate cause; wrong choice, persistence in wrong, and wilful self-destruction. Nothing in *Macbeth* allows us to find a cause in the terrible doctrine of Calvin by which God predestinates man to reprobation and in so doing wills those sins for which he is damned. But Shakespeare has presented the thing itself, the hardening of heart or incapacity for penitence on which so many preachers dwelt, and for which Calvin provided so ghastly an explanation.

In *King Lear* Shakespeare deliberately took an opposite course. He set his play, which in his source was set in a Christian world, in a pagan world. It is unhistoric, or outside history. It is a world of gods, not of revealed religion; but it is also not a world of religious rites, ceremonies and duties. This makes *King Lear* unique among the tragedies, and unique, I think, among modern tragedies. We are not confronted with ancient Romans or modern Danes, or ancient Britons, for that matter. (*King Lear* presents a very difficult problem to the producer who has to decide on what kind of clothes the characters should wear.) Shakespeare must have made this decision deliberately. It gave him a freedom he enjoyed in no other play; and in no other play do the characters so constantly invoke, exclaim against, or attempt to characterize the 'powers' that rule the world. In this play, of all his plays, Shakespeare seems concerned with the mystery of things, 'the heavy and the weary weight of all this unintelligible world'. No play has more tempted the 'Christian critics'. No play has been more seized on to prove Shakespeare's profound agnosticism, his deeply pessimistic attitude to the course of affairs, to how the world wags. The design of *King Lear* is unlike the design of *Hamlet* and *Macbeth*. It is differently seen by different characters. At the close there is no summation of what we have seen comparable to Horatio's summation of the devious plot of *Hamlet*, nor is there any judgment expressed with the firmness of the judgment at the close of *Macbeth*. Textually, it is uncertain who speaks the final words, Albany or Edgar. But the point is immaterial, for Albany, the just man, believes in heaven's justice, and Edgar is throughout the play's philosopher. If the end of *King Lear* could be moralized, these are of all the characters those who could moralize it. But *King Lear*, like *Othello*, does not end with any interpretation of what we have seen. *Othello* ends by pointing us to 'the tragic loading of this bed' and to Iago: 'This is thy work.' *King Lear* ends with the simple recognition of the immensity of Lear's suffering and endurance. 'The oldest hath borne most', and with the warning that we should 'speak what we feel, not what we ought to say', as if Shakespeare were asking us not to respond to his play with any formulas. Some years ago I suggested that the difficulty of analysing *Othello*, which has made some call it 'a tragedy without meaning', was that it includes two designs: the tragic movement towards a final catastrophic action, and the comic movement through misunderstanding to the discovery of truth and the reunion of those whom misunderstanding has separated.[1] *King Lear* is similarly inclusive. It has, as Professor Edwards[2] has said, the three-part structure of the great comedies: initial sundering; separation, the central stage of bewilderment where identities are confused, the blasted heath being a terrible version of the Wood near Athens or the Forest of Arden; and meeting and reconciliation. But to this comic pattern, the pattern of his source and of all other versions of the story,[3] Shakespeare has added an appalling coda: the shocking death of Cordelia. These twin peaks of human experience, as Professor Edwards has called them, confront each other: the moment when 'all losses are restored and sorrows end', and the moment of absolute loss. The moral

[1] 'The Noble Moor', *Proceedings of the British Academy* (1956).
[2] Philip Edwards, *Shakespeare and the Confines of Art* (1968), pp. 129–33.
[3] It is sometimes argued that Shakespeare softened his source by having Cordelia hanged in prison, since in the sources she hanged herself years after Lear's death when imprisoned by her sisters' sons who had rebelled against her. But this is not part of the story of Lear which, in all versions but Shakespeare's, ends with his restoration to the throne and his finding his rest in Cordelia's 'kind nursery'. It is not Cordelia's death that is shocking but her death at this moment.

climate of *King Lear*, unlike the moral climate of *Hamlet*, is without ambiguity. We are left in no doubt who are good and who are bad, and know clearly what is wrong and what is right action. The mystery here is not in man's nature or in the dubieties of the conscience, but in the nature of things. No single statement of the many that are made upon the course of things in the world sums up the play's course. But none can be ignored. All have some measure of truth. There is judgment: it is seen in the destruction of the wicked by their own lawless appetites, in the retribution that so swiftly cuts down Cornwall, and in the formal ordeal by battle between Edgar and Edmund. There is the power of Fortune, of which a king reduced to beggary has always been the great symbol: it is felt throughout the play, most at its close when the good that Edmund meant to do is done too late, as the Friar's message to Romeo was delayed by accident. But the Wheel of Fortune is also a Wheel of Fire, burning away dross and discovering the ore, testing the common coinage of life to separate false from true. *King Lear* presents an extremity of suffering, physical and mental, falling on man from the hostility of the natural world, the cruelty of others, the visitations of fortune, and the burning shame the thought of his own sins and follies brings. It displays suffering as the universal law of life with all the heightening of common experience that tragedy gives. But without in any way diminishing agony and pain it shows men discovering through their suffering truth, and beyond its demonstration of learning by suffering, the *to pathein mathein* of the Aeschylean tragedy of suffering, it displays most movingly the fellowship of suffering, that men are bound to each other in their pain. As the play proceeds the prosperous fall apart; the outcasts draw together, sharing each other's burdens and bearing their griefs. *King Lear* presents no answer to the great question why this world is as it is. Yet I cannot think it irreligious or un-Christian to present an image of the universe which can sustain as partially true so many of the affirmations men have made about the world we are born into, and which, since none is adequate to the range and depth of our experience, confronts us at the close with the ultimate mystery of death.

Johnson did not object to the death of Cordelia on the grounds
that a play in which 'the virtuous miscarry is not a just representation of the common events of human life', but because the spectacle was too distressing, and thus disappointed the expectation of
pleasure which brought men to the theatre. His noble review of
Soame Jenyns's presumptuous attempt to decide 'upon questions
out of the reach of human determination'[1] reveals his outrage at
the notion that the workings of the divine economy are visible in
the world of human experience or can be demonstrated to our
reason. He knew well that in life there is no 'poetical justice' and
that this world provides no answer to 'the problem of pain'. As
Eliot's mouthpiece, Agatha, says in *The Family Reunion*, 'In this
world it is inexplicable'. If there is any answer it lies in another
world than the world of which the tragic poet presents an image.

[1] In his *Free Inquiry into the Nature and Origin of Evil* (1757), reviewed
by Johnson in three consecutive numbers of the *Literary Magazine*; see
Works, vi, and R. T. Davies, *Selected Writings* (1965), which prints the
most powerful passages.

IV

The Concept of the Tragic Today

The subject-matter of tragedy is certain permanent features of human life; but tragedy is an exceedingly rare plant. Like its near companion, epic, it appears to require a certain soil or climate. In this it is unlike comedy, which is a hardy perennial. If, as I have said, the very phrase 'great tragedy' is a tautology, the phrase 'great comedy' is not. It is not absurd to praise a comedy as 'mildly amusing'; it would be ludicrous to say of a tragedy that it was 'mildly moving'. Tragedy has to succeed greatly if it is to succeed at all. Rudimentary comedy amuses: its effect is comparable to that of great comedy. It makes us laugh, and sends us away pleased and happy, feeling that the world is manageable, if we are sensible, and that other people are less sensible than we are, which is gratifying. And even if it makes us aware of some follies of our own, they are harmless and corrigible follies. But rudimentary tragedy does not move. As melodrama it may excite suspense and give us the easy gratifications of applauding virtue and hissing vice; but the painful pleasure, the tragic sense of pity and fear, the discovery of human greatness in human weakness and of human nobility in human error and crime, the experience of being at once deeply moved and calm, involved and not involved, and of feeling that we are in some degree seeing into the truth of things—these are something different in kind, and not merely in degree, from the excitements of melodrama, or from the physical and nervous thrills of Grand Guignol and its modern descendants. And if we turn from rudimentary and unsophisticated 'tragedy' to plays that eschew these easy ways of dealing with the terrible and the pathetic, and attempt to present the matter of tragedy with tragic dignity, the vast majority not only fail to move: they succeed only too well in boring. Outside brief periods in fifth-century Athens, Elizabethan and Jacobean London, and seventeenth-century Paris, virtually all the plays that call themselves 'Tragedies', and were admired as such in their own day, can be read only by devoted and determined literary historians.

Comedy has a steady and traceable development. Relations are visible between classical comedy and its imitations at the Renaissance, and links between them are provided by the farces that developed into the *Commedia dell'Arte*. A history of comedy is a history of growth and evolution. Restoration comedy grows out of Caroline, as if the theatres had never been closed; and out of this, by a natural reaction, comes sentimental and domestic comedy. Through all the changes certain comic themes and comic situations persist and are always amusing, as are many comic personages and types. The *nouveau riche*, the pretentious gallant, the unsuccessful wit are permanent social types however much the social standards they fail to reach may vary. The braggart, the pedant, the clever rogue, the fashionable lady, the persons who in some way 'do not belong', or 'do not see the point', although idioms and fashions and clothes change, and the groups they fail to belong to have different characteristics, are immediately recognizable as familiar and provoke laughter. By historical verisimilitude, by holding up the mirror to the ordinary, the everyday, the contingent, the comic writer hits the universal and shows us Man in men. Comedy, apparently unambitious of dealing with the eternal verities, delighting in the topical and evanescent, finding its subject in 'the harmless follies of the time', shows us follies that are of all time. It wears extremely well and even improves and matures with age. The topicality that delighted contemporary playgoers is part of the secret of its appeal to posterity, convincing us of its actuality and giving us the pleasure of recognizing the *idem in alio*. It is precisely this pleasure that we lack when we turn to tragedies written outside the great ages. Far from responding to a representation of the permanent passions of men and seeing a reflection in the manners and idiom, of another age of our own aspirations and defeats, we find it difficult to believe that human beings can ever have felt these emotions, exhibited this behaviour or expressed these sentiments, or that audiences could ever have been moved to tears or applause at these fictive griefs and this extravagant highmindedness.

Outside Greek, Elizabethan and French Classical Tragedy, no so-called tragedies survive in repertory and very few attract amateurs. Such elementary comedies as *Ralph Roister Doister* and *Gammer Gurton's Needle* can still amuse on a warm summer's night in a college garden; but not even undergraduates would dream of staging *Gorboduc*. Restoration Comedy delights as long as one does not see too much of it. With the possible exception of Otway's *Venice Preserved*, Restoration Tragedy is dead. Dryden's *All for Love* has a kind of posthumous life in university syllabuses. The two performances that I have sat through hovered uncertainly between the tedious and the ludicrous. The eighteenth century, not a period notable for drama, provides some classic comedies. Not even an amateur company would attempt to stage Addison's *Cato* or Johnson's *Irene*, the one highly thought of in its own day, the other a failure. Yet one would have thought that Johnson, of all writers, had the tragic writer's sense of life's pain and the tragic writer's uncompromising moral sternness. All the great romantic poets attempted to write tragedies, as did Tennyson, with some success at the time, and Browning. Their plays are unactable, though the generous spirit of Professor Wilson Knight thinks Byron's tragedies worthy of production; they are also, with the possible exception of *The Cenci*, unreadable. We read them, if at all, not for their own merits but for the light they throw on their authors' ideas in their other works. At the close of the nineteenth century Stephen Phillips gained a stupendous reputation as a dramatic and tragic poet. It is a melancholy experience to turn from the tributes to his genius to a reading of his dramas. Any history of the drama will provide titles of tragedies admired in their own day, unactable and unreadable now. The immense prestige of tragedy made it an *ignis fatuus*, like the idea of the heroic poem as 'the noblest work of man', or the fatal attraction of King Arthur as a national poetic hero. It lured poet after poet to attempt the impossible: to manufacture, out of literary ideals and critical theories and the ambition to scale the heights, works that should equal masterpieces of imaginative power. They reveal at once their factitiousness.

If it is argued that in the eighteenth and nineteenth centuries the drama in England had declined and that the novel had replaced it as the chief mode for the imaginative presentation of human life, there are still extremely few novels, if we abandon the idea that a tragedy must be cast in dramatic form, that can be regarded as unquestionably tragic. The progeny of Fielding has been far more numerous than the progeny of Richardson, who in *Clarissa* succeeded in creating in the novel a work 'of the Tragic Kind'. *The Bride of Lammermuir*, *Wuthering Heights*, *Tess of the D'Urbervilles*, *The Mayor of Casterbridge* would probably occur in most lists. But apart from these, there would be little agreement and any list would be a short one. It might similarly be argued that, although most tragedies which have been inspired by the desire to emulate the tragic masterpieces of antiquity or of Shakespeare are dead, the 'tragic sense of life', or the 'tragic vision', has found expression in many plays in this century, which though very different from Shakespearian Tragedy, as Shakespearian Tragedy is very different from Greek, deserve to be called 'modern tragedies'. Yet I doubt very much whether it would be possible to find any large measure of agreement on which modern plays could properly be called tragedies, and so much discussion of 'modern tragedy' resolves itself into a justification of the use of the term as to suggest that 'modern tragedy' is an unreal category. However much *Hamlet* differs from the *Oresteia* nobody doubts that both are tragedies and need no qualifying adjectives. But even those plays by the great Scandinavians, Ibsen and Strindberg, which have the strongest claim to be regarded as modern tragedies, lack the sense of life as potentially glorious that gives the catastrophes of tragedy their special poignancy, and even more the tragic eloquence that Hume thought the secret of tragedy's pleasure.

[*93*]

To speak therefore of 'The Death of Tragedy', as if tragedy were an art-form which after flourishing through the ages had withered and perished in modern times, or to enquire why certain ages, including our own, have not produced tragedy, as if this were a matter of reproach to them, ignores literary history and is to ask the wrong question. It is the birth, rapid growth and quick exhaustion of this rare form that is the phenomenon that needs explanation. The real question is why, at certain brief periods and in certain places, these masterpieces of the human imagination appeared. For, as well as being rare in time, tragedy is rare in place. It is a European phenomenon. Other civilizations do not seem to have felt the urge to isolate 'the dark side for contemplation' and to find meaning in the chances, changes and disasters of mortal life. And as it would be absurd to pass judgment on civilizations and cultures which have not produced tragedy, so, when I argue for a relation between tragedy and religion, I am not suggesting any judgment on the religious experience and religious thought of cultures and ages in which tragedy has not flowered. The argument is not that one age is more religious than another and that the 'Death of Tragedy' is a consequence of a decline in religion; but that there is a relation between tragedy and the dominant religious conceptions of the ages in which it appeared, and that the dominant religious conceptions of other ages are reflected in the absence of tragedy, or in the production of works that we regard as either not fully tragic or as tragic *pastiche*.

A sharp and crude distinction can be made between two attitudes that a religious spirit may take towards the chances, changes and calamities of this life. They may be regarded as proof of the essential transitoriness and unsatisfactoriness of earthly existence, teaching us to place our hope in another world, and to see men's sorrows, errors and crimes as springing from their absorption in this world, and their slavery to the body and its passions, affections and needs. Redemption is then seen as man's progressive emancipation from the wheel of time and the bondage of the flesh by discipline, detachment and prayer; so that, while still living in the body, he lives more and more in the spirit, which is the only reality, all else being only 'a muddy vesture of decay'. Or, on the other hand, suffering and calamity can be seen as the consequence of universal sin, and this world can be regarded as something in itself good which has gone terribly wrong, so that the whole creation is 'groaning and travailing'. Suffering is then to be accepted and endured, and even welcomed, as an offering by which we are made one again with God, bearing one another's as well as our own burdens in union with a divine Saviour, who shares with us the consequences of sin and its pain. These two religious attitudes towards experience, the mystical and the Christian, are not mutually exclusive and impervious to each other. They have interpenetrated each other in history. Both depend on a common religious assumption: that the world is not self-explanatory. The unproved and unprovable assumption of faith is that the world into which we are born and in which we live and die is not the final world: that there is another world 'on the other side of things'.

Yet there is a radical difference. The mystical conception, fundamental in the great religions of the East, of the soul as imprisoned in matter, and of redemption as salvation and escape from the world of time and the flesh, is incompatible with the sense that all our experience in this world has value and meaning which would seem to inspire the tragic poet. Doctrines of reincarnation are inconsistent with tragic finality and completeness, as are doctrines of eternal recurrence, which see human life as a pattern of ebb and flow, in terms of return and renewal. These resemble the comic pattern of the continual flow of life, of decay and renewal through the generations, not the tragic pattern of resolution in a final conclusion. Religions which preach withdrawal from the world of human action, and train the human spirit in detachment from its fellows, teaching it to aspire towards 'the flight of the Alone to the Alone', or to the bliss of Nirvana, put aside the tragic questions, and will not inspire artists to find meaning in human life in its short course in this world of illusion.

It is sometimes said that the Christian doctrine of a life in the world to come, and of reward and punishment after death is equally destructive of tragic finality, and that nobody who really believed these doctrines could write a tragedy. This is a curious notion. The concept of rewards and punishments after death is held very strongly in other religions than the Christian, nor is Christianity unique in believing in an after-life. Its uniqueness lies, as I have said, in the doctrine of the Resurrection: 'Behold I make all things new.' Tragedy presents the historical, the course of life in this world. Nobody has ever suggested that Sophocles's play *The Women of Trachis* is not profoundly and terribly tragic because the audience, like the author, knew that Heracles was rewarded for his labours and apotheosized. It is not suggested that they all went home saying his agony did not really matter, consoled by the thought that after his death he was taken to Olympus and made a god. The after-life of Heracles is not part of the subject of *The Women of Trachis*. It is as irrelevant as the 'damnation' of Othello, of which we have heard so much, or any reunion of Lear and Cordelia beyond the grave, of which mercifully we have heard less. Even in tragedies that are in the full sense Christian tragedies, written to promulgate Christian truths, such as *Samson Agonistes* or *Murder in the Cathedral*, we are still equally confined to this world. We know that Samson is forgiven and that his repentance has won acceptance because he has been given strength to destroy the Philistines, and by so doing has renewed the faith and courage of Israel, not because he is taken up into heaven and rewarded there. Milton has chosen as his subject an exceptional event, a 'sign'. It is something quite outside the usual order of things in this world where 'patience is more oft the exercise of Saints'. In *Murder in the Cathedral* this patience of the martyr is the subject, a victory that is not of this world. Again it is not Thomas's reward in heaven that confirms his victory, but the demonstration that the blood of the martyrs is the seed of the Church expressed in the final chorus of praise and thanksgiving by the women of Canterbury. Nobody ever believed more strongly in the justice of the recompense that virtue and vice will receive after death than Samuel Richardson. It could be claimed that it was precisely the strength of his faith that gave him the courage not to spare Clarissa. 'Spare her, Mr.

Richardson, spare her virtue', wrote Mrs. Pilkington, herself she disarmingly owned a lady of easy virtue. Along with Mr. Colley Cibber she could not bear to think that the beautiful and virtuous Clarissa should endure rape. But Richardson went doggedly on to his appalling conclusion, where 'No voice divine the storm allayed, No light propitious shone', to what he described as 'The supposed Tragical (tho' I think *Triumphant*) Catastrophe' in which virtue is its own reward and vice its own damnation. 'A writer', Richardson wrote, 'who follows Nature and pretends to keep the Christian System in his Eye, cannot make a Heaven in this World for his Favourites: or represent this Life otherwise than as a State of Probation.'[1] Tragedy concerns itself with this world, with what we know and can imagine, with what is visible to sight and known to our experience. In the design of its plot, and in comment in chorus and by characters, metaphysical and religious ideas are given expression; but the world it presents has the obscurity and the mystery of the world we live in. In this obscurity and mystery it touches the world of religious experience and feeling, as in its design and its conceptualizations it employs religious formulations.

'Religion', wrote von Hügel, 'is dim—in the religious temper there should be a great simplicity, and a certain contentedness in dimness. . . . God does not make our lives all shipshape, clear and comfortable. Never try to get things too clear. Religion can't be clear. In this mixed-up life there is always an element of unclearness. I believe God wills it so. There is always an element of tragedy. . . . When I was a young man I was always interested in religion, in the facts of religion, and I felt these facts to be outside of myself, not my imagination. As far as I can see them, they are quite beyond my imagination. If I could understand religion as I understand that two and two make four, it would not be worth my understanding. Religion can't be clear if it is worth having.'[2] 'We know what we are, but we do not know what we may be', says Ophelia in her madness. (It sounds so like a text of Scripture

---

[1] *Letter to Lady Bradshaigh*, 15th December 1748.
[2] *Letters to a Niece* (1928), pp. xvi–xvii.

that it is a surprise not to find it in the Concordance.) By faith men believe in a life in the world to come; but that life is unimaginable. We can present symbols for it: they remain symbols pointing beyond themselves to something beyond experience and imagination. If we can say 'I know that all things work together for good for them that love God', this is knowledge of a different kind from the knowledge that enables us to say 'I know that all men die'. If we attempt to demonstrate the first kind of knowledge in individual lives, or in the course of history, both heart and mind will revolt at the callousness of the calculation. A Christian who is told that his faith protects him from experience of the tragic has a good defence. The servant is not greater than his master, nor the disciple than his Lord. The Lord on earth saw no special providence in the fall of the tower of Siloam where the innocent perished with the guilty; he wept over the grave of his friend Lazarus, not rejoicing that he had passed from this transitory world to life eternal; he wept over the doomed city of Jerusalem, not seeing in its fall merely a punishment for its sins; he was troubled in soul and body in Gethsemane and longed, like his fellow-men, that he might not have to drink the bitter cup of death; upon the Cross he knew the sense of being abandoned, of the withdrawal of the sense of the presence of God in his extremest need. The course of individual lives and of world history is as mysterious and painful to the imagination of a Christian as to any human imagination. But the existence of the doctrine of the Resurrection, and of belief in the sovereignty of Christ, and in an over-ruling Providence bringing good out of evil, and ordering all things finally for good, are not, I think, irrelevant to the rebirth of tragedy in Christian Europe.

The doctrine of the Resurrection—the re-creation of the total personality as it has been known and as it has known itself on earth—makes the acts and words of individual man here in his flesh of eternal significance. It declares that at death the soul does not enter on another stage of its earthly pilgrimage, nor escape from the prison of the body and the burden of individuality by absorption into the eternal life of the One, as a water drop is dissolved into the ocean, nor attain Nirvana. It faces judgment. That judgment is on a man's whole life, on what he has made of himself when he comes to die. The doctrine of Providence asserts that this world is ordered, that nothing that happens in it is irrelevant and that, however it appears to us, to God there is no accident. The doctrine of special Providence—that not a sparrow falls to the ground without the Father and that the very hairs of our head are numbered—asserts that the same is true of each individual life. There is purpose and pattern in the whole scheme of things and in the life of every man. At the centre of its thought and devotion the Christian religion has a single human life, historically lived and historically recorded and ending with death and burial. The early Church fought and rejected the doctrine that this was not a true human life and a true death, that it was a phantom that suffered on the Cross in place of the impassible Son of God, and that the Crucifixion was a kind of sacred farce in which an 'Actor on the Tree'

> *Would loll at ease, miming pain*
> *And counterfeit mortality.*[1]

In the twelfth century, in the terrible cruelties and horrors of the Albigensian Crusade, the battle was fought again between the belief that God was the God of this world and that the Son of God truly died upon the Cross to redeem it, and the belief that the true God was without this world, which was the creation of an Evil God and was irredeemable. In its emphasis on the value of the individual and its assertion of the importance and irreversability of historic events Christianity, of all the highly developed religions, can best accommodate tragic experience as relevant to man's quest for truth and reality.

Why for a certain brief period of time Greek religious feeling was able to create out of the most painful and terrible aspects of human experience coherent and beautiful works of art which still satisfy the imagination by their truth to life, and speak to the heart and conscience; and why some two thousand years later, in

[1] Edwin Muir, 'The Recurrence', *Collected Poems* (1960), p. 104.

Elizabethan England, the Christian belief in judgment and in Providence and the Christian acceptance of suffering as not only punitive but as potentially redemptive, if not directly inspiring dramatists, provided a climate which allowed a brief flowering of works comparable in scope, profundity and beauty are questions that caution suggests it might be better not to ask, since satisfactory answers are unlikely to be found. But it is possible to suggest parallels in the sixteenth century to conditions that have been thought contributory to the appearance of tragedy in fifth-century Athens.

The roots of Greek tragedy are generally recognized to lie in developments in Greek religious feeling in the Archaic Age, the sixth century B.C., the age lying between the world of Homer and the world of Aeschylus. As Professor Dodds[1] has said, old beliefs came to arouse new and powerful religious emotions: 'there is a deepened awareness of human insecurity and human helplessness, which has its religious correlate in the feeling of divine hostility.' Attempts are made to moralize this divine 'jealousy', and to make the gods, particularly Zeus, agents of justice punishing the guilty, to discover in the felt hostility of the gods some moral principle by which the arbitrary can be seen as the just. The dominant religious emotion thus becomes the sense of guilt; and the dominant religious need, the need for purification. But guilt is not limited to those who have committed guilty acts: it spreads by infection and can be inherited as a curse. The dread of pollution is universal and brings a widespread growth of rituals of purification. This becomes the main religious concern of the greatest of Greek shrines, the Oracle at Delphi. Professor Dodds, borrowing the terms from American anthropologists, calls the culture of the Archaic Age a 'Guilt Culture' and the culture of the Homeric Age a 'Shame Culture'. In a 'Shame Culture' what men most desire is fame, the esteem of their fellows, and what they most dread is

[1] See E. R. Dodds, *The Greeks and the Irrational* (1951), Chapter II, 'From Shame-Culture to Guilt-Culture', which I have summarized. But I am indebted to Professor Dodds's profound and beautiful book throughout.

loss of honour. In a 'Guilt Culture' what men most long for is release from the burden of guilt, quiet of conscience, and what they most dread is the sense of alienation from others and all the oppressive anxiety implied in the words 'a sense of guilt'. Professor Dodds, while agreeing that we must remember that Homer was writing for an aristocratic military culture and no doubt, therefore, in order to please his patrons ignored traditional beliefs and practices that did not commend themselves to the wealthy and the warlike; and while accepting that 'general social conditions' made the Archaic Age in Mainland Greece a 'time of extreme personal insecurity', would hazard a further suggestion. He sees the domination of the sense of guilt as arising from the clash between the growing claims of the individual to personal rights and personal responsibilities and the claims of the family. Religious feeling and religious sanctions, conservative as always, supported the family, and particularly the power and authority of the Father. He suggests that from the tensions of family life and the repressed desires of the children for freedom there arose strong feelings of guilt which were projected into the religious sphere.

Parallels can be drawn between the temper of the Archaic Age and the temper of the later Middle Ages. In theology there had developed that legalistic theory of the Atonement which saw Christ as suffering the punishment that the sins of men deserved, and interpreted the Crucifixion not as a victory over the powers of darkness, by payment of a ransom that rescued mankind from sin and death, but as a satisfaction made to the offended justice of the Father. This Anselmian doctrine, which supplanted earlier and rival doctrines and became orthodox, interpreted Christ's reconciliation of man to God through his death in legal and mercantile terms, as payment of a debt that man could himself never pay. It made of original sin original guilt. Its dominance is reflected in the concentration of Western Art of the later Middle Ages on the Cross; the Crucified Saviour is the focus of devotion, not the Risen Lord. It makes of the Mass primarily, and almost exclusively, the Holy Sacrifice, propitiatory, offered for the sins of the world, of the living and the dead. The sense of the burden of sin brings the development of the doctrine of purgatory and, in the fifteenth century, the proliferation of chantries devoted to the offering of Masses for the dead, the growth of indulgences, and the ramifications of the penitential system. The characteristic tympanum of a Romanesque West Door will show Christ in glory, surrounded by the symbols of the evangelists, with the apostles sitting calm and dignified in a row beneath. The West Door of a Gothic Cathedral shows something very different, not Christ in Glory but Christ in Judgment, the spectacle of the *Dies Irae*, the Day of Wrath. The obsession with death, the moment of individual judgment, in the later Middle Ages I have dwelt on earlier. It would perhaps be possible to suggest, as Professor Dodds has done, a sociological explanation of this stress on guilt and judgment in the crumbling of feudal society, based on personal bonds and loyalties, and in the change from a fundamentally rural economy to a mercantile, disturbing old patterns of life and breaking old ties and old prohibitions; but I am not a sociologist. All I wish to stress is that as the 'Guilt Culture' of the Archaic Age lies behind the appearance of Attic Tragedy, so the growing obsession of the religious imagination and of religious thought and devotion with sin and death and judgment in the later Middle Ages lies behind Elizabethan Tragedy, providing what Professor Gombrich has taught us to call the *schemata* by correction of which great artists explore the world.

It lies behind. Greek Tragedy is not the product of the Archaic Age, but of the age that comes after, and Elizabethan Tragedy is not a product of the later Middle Ages but of the Renaissance. I am not arguing to put Shakespeare back into the late medieval world, and for Eliot's Shakespeare, making do with the 'mixed and muddled scepticism of the Renaissance', substituting a Shakespeare affirming old orthodoxies. But I think that these stern and sombre conceptions provided him with his first 'sketches' as it were. I would lean here on Professor Gombrich's distinction between medieval and postmedieval art. There is no doubt on which side of this divide Shakespeare stands:

To the Middle Ages, the schema is the image; to the post-medieval artist, it is the starting point for corrections, adjustments, adaptations, the means to probe reality and to wrestle with the particular. The hallmark of the medieval artist is the firm line that testifies to the mastery of his craft. That of the postmedieval artist is not facility, which he avoids, but constant alertness. Its symptom is the sketch, or rather the many sketches which precede the finished work and, for all the skill of hand and eye that marks the master, a constant readiness to learn, to make and to match and remake till the portrayal ceases to be a secondhand formula and reflects the unique and unrepeatable experience the artist wishes to seize and hold.

It is this constant search, this sacred discontent, which constitutes the leaven of the Western mind since the Renaissance and pervades our art no less than our science. For it is not only the scientist . . . who can examine the schema and test its validity. Since the time of Leonardo, at least, every great artist has done the same, consciously, or unconsciously.[1]

Professor Gombrich is concerned with the art of the presentation of the illusion of reality on a flat surface, applying to the artist Karl Popper's conception of the scientist as ceaselessly making and mending, testing hypothesis and formula constantly against experience. It can be applied to Shakespeare, a ceaseless experimenter in the art of the presentation of the illusion of actual human experience within the limits of 'the two hours traffic' of his stage.

If we are to attempt an answer to the question why tragedy appears in Elizabethan England, we have first to accept that genius is not explicable in terms of causes and is a kind of miraculous accident. If Shakespeare had died in the great plague of 1592–3 it seems highly unlikely that we should be speaking of the Jacobean Age as a great age of tragic drama and comparing it with fifth-century Athens. The other dramatists, as it is, are really carried on his back; and, if Shakespeare had never lived to be, as modern scholarship holds, again and again the innovator, creating new possibilities for his contemporaries and successors, there might well have been no Jacobean tragedy thought worthy of the

---

[1] E. H. Gombrich, *Art and Illusion* (1960), pp. 173–4.

title. But granted the inexplicability of genius, the possibilities open to genius are conditioned by inheritance from the past and the opportunities of the present. Like all other human phenomena genius is historically conditioned. If we ask 'Why Tragedy?', there is a related question: 'Why Science?' There is a great leap here too. Why suddenly, after centuries, do so many great and fruitful hypotheses about the natural world appear in all fields of knowledge? If there is a parallel between the religious temper of the Archaic Age and the temper of the later Middle Ages, there is also a parallel between the achievements of Ionian science and the scientific Renaissance in sixteenth-century Europe. In both ancient Greece and modern Europe the age of tragedy is succeeded by the age of the triumph of science or natural philosophy, to give it its older and better name, a triumph whose origins lie much further back. All theories of tragedy, as I have said, speak in various terms of reconcilement, of the co-existence in tragic art of contraries which seem irreconcilable; and interpretations of any tragedy swing between two poles. For tragedy displays causes in calamities and shows design, but in so doing reveals what remains mysterious and inexplicable. I cannot believe that such works originate in scepticism, or in perplexities, or confusion, or from that 'metaphysical despair' which is what the 'tragic sense' or 'the tragic vision' has come to mean today. On the contrary, I believe that the tragic poet is inspired by confidence in man's power to understand the world of historic experience, the same spirit that attempts to discover by hypothesis and experiment the laws that govern the physical world. His hypotheses are the religious conceptions that dominate the imagination of his age. These direct his imagination to the material it works on and with the aid of these he shapes his plot: but the material, the stories of guilt and suffering, of crime and retribution, of catastrophe overwhelming the innocent, and of 'purposes mistook', has not been invented to exemplify: on the contrary, men most desire to find meaning in stories of this kind because they most test the assumption that the world is rationally ordered.

In recent years many dramatists have been concerned with what are some of the main elements in tragic art: cruelty, violence of all kinds, madness, and sexual frenzy. Others, who are not attracted by the more sensational and horrifying outbursts of savagery and irrationality in man, are concerned with a painful sense of meaninglessness. It is, I suppose, because I am a child of my time that I have stressed so much the irrational and mysterious in tragedy where in earlier centuries men stressed the sequence of cause and effect. Where many nineteenth-century scholars stressed rationality, the stress today is on the irrational. Verrall's *Euripides the Rationalist* has become Professor Dodds's 'Euripides the Irrationalist'.[1] Professor Dodds is not claiming that Euripides was not a rationalist, but that he was aware of the power of the irrational, which no rationalist can ignore, and is concerned to reveal this in all its terror and beauty, not to expose superstition and its dangers. But today the irrational and the mysterious has become the whole of what men mean when they speak of 'the tragic': violence on the one hand, confusion and meaninglessness on the other. A few years ago, Robert Lowell put this very clearly. He was commenting on the fact that he felt there was something 'phoney' about President Kennedy's patronage of the arts. He said he felt this acutely when he was present at a party where the President was entertaining a group of poets, as if poetry were something that really mattered, and was serious and important. Then he was suddenly called from the room for a while, and next day it was clear that during his short absence he had had to take some big decision. Lowell commented:

> The arts are in a very funny position now. . . . We are free to say what we want to, and somehow what we want to say is the confusion and sadness and incoherence of the human condition. Anyone running a government must say the opposite of that: that it can be solved. He must take an optimistic stance. I don't know why the arts say this so strongly. It may be a more miserable time, more than others, with the world liable to blow up. We're in some transition domestically: I mean in one's family and everything else. There are new moral

[1] The title of an article by Professor Dodds in the *Classical Review* (1929).

possibilities; new moral incoherence. It's a very confused moment. And for some reason it's almost a dogma with us: art must show confusion.[1]

Tragedy is by definition the imitation of an action that is complete. Finality is its essence. The most famous and, many would say, the most significant play of our day is a play in which, to use a famous distinction of Eliot's, things happen but there is no event. Nobody could possibly call *Waiting for Godot* a tragedy, not on such trivial grounds as that it is about tramps and is often very funny, but because nothing occurs in it to surprise or to satisfy our expectation and there is really no reason inherent in it why it should not go on for ever. As a work of art it is neither tragic nor pathetic, however much it may be said to embody the modern 'tragic vision'. It has been unsympathetically described as presenting 'a world of repartee and symbolic props stimulating our minds rather than our emotions, so that we are left neither exalted nor depressed but full of metaphysical questions.'[2] More sympathetically it has been called a modern *Everyman*, that is to say a morality play, written to express a view of life, not to discover meaning in the presentation of what gives us the illusion of an actual event. It takes place, like all moral plays, in a no-man's-land at an unspecified time. Eugene O'Neill attempted to write modern tragedies in such plays as *Desire under the Elms* and his long trilogy *Mourning Becomes Electra*. These seem pretentious and over-literary in conception and ineloquent compared with his two final masterpieces: *The Iceman Cometh* and *The Long Day's Journey into Night*. Here we have a very powerful illusion of historic actuality, of the here and now. But here again there is a total lack of climax, an absence of event, and in both plays there is no resolution but a relapse into a dream world of fantasies. *The Long Day's Journey into Night* is almost intolerably moving in the theatre. In it O'Neill abandoned the attempt to find an objective correlative for his belief that love is the source of all our suffering,

[1] *Encounter* (February 1965).
[2] David McCutchion, in an article on 'Tragedy and Pathos', *Jadavpur Journal of Comparative Literature*, Vol. VI (1966).

and presented what is virtually his own life-story. If the characters did not love each other, were not bound together as a family, they would not hurt each other or be hurt, destroy and be destroyed. The play communicates with immense pathos a sense of absolute hopelessness, of 'might have been, no more, too late, farewell'. The drunken failure of a father, with his shoddy theatrical rhetoric, living on his memory and his fantasy of himself as a great actor, the angry drunken elder son, the consumptive younger son, the poet, the mother who has escaped from life into the dream world of drugs, and remembers in her drugged wanderings at the close the happy and hopeful innocence of her convent girlhood: these are defeated and find no meaning in their defeat. They present the pattern of a net of destructive impulses in which they are all caught. Unable to escape, they console themselves with dreams of what never was and what might have been, fantasies of a happiness and success never possessed, and schemes of what may yet be done, which are revealed as futile when the mother appears at the close. She has relapsed from the effort to face the intolerable present into the safety of a drugged vision of the past. There is no terror here: only an almost unbearable sadness.

It is too facile to say that this sense of 'no pattern' and retreat from all we mean by 'plot' is to be explained by absence of religious faith. It is not confined to non-believers. It appears conspicuously in Eliot's one attempt at pure tragedy, *The Family Reunion*. This is concerned with an event that never took place: the hero's non-murder of his wife. It is Harry in *The Family Reunion* who makes the distinction between happenings and events, saying that 'those to whom nothing has ever happened cannot understand the unimportance of events'. He is referring to his poor, baffled uncles and aunts, with their thirst to listen to the news, 'the weather report and the international catastrophes'. As Agatha informs us, *The Family Reunion* is not a story of crime and punishment but of sin and expiation. It turns what we are accustomed to see in tragedy inside out. This is clear from the remarkable handling of the chorus. It would be rash to attempt to interpret any Greek tragedy solely by the comments of the chorus, and the statement that the chorus exists to provide an 'ideal spectator' is plainly an inadequate summary of its very diverse functions in different plays. Even so, the chorus in *The Family Reunion* reaches a *ne plus ultra* of incomprehension. One can hardly blame them for turning for relief to listen to the news, since Harry offers to their contemplation merely inexplicable behaviour instead of actions whose import demands interpretation and calls for judgment.

On a different level from plays with no events, we have more recently been exposed to the theatre of cruelty, of events for events' sake, with no meaning; as if the only reality was physical reality, the touch of flesh on flesh, the crack of bone on bone. This is regarded as the 'thing itself', the real. Shakespeare's plays have been cut and slashed to conform to this ideal. We have seen productions of the Histories in which executions and hangings *coram populo* seemed the main point; and, instead of a few persons with 'rusty blades' simulating York and Lancaster's 'long jars', we have been given mock gladiatorial shows. In a much-praised production of *King Lear* the terrible spectacle of Gloucester's blinding was not balanced by any of the acts of mercy, pity and love which Shakespeare's image of human life also included. In defiance of the text, Cornwall's servants, instead of fetching flax and white of eggs to apply to his bleeding eyes and leading him to the Bedlamite, pushed him about the stage, as blood appeared in great gouts on the piece of muslin thrown over his head, in a hideous blindman-hoodman's buff. Edmund was not allowed any final act of good against his nature, and a stony little Cordelia was as dry-eyed as the audience. This highly acclaimed production evacuated *King Lear* of all moral feeling and presented an image of almost unrelieved savagery, violence and craziness.

Some see in the theatre of cruelty a reflection of the horrors of twentieth-century wars and revolutions, darkening the imagination and imposing on individuals a sense of utter powerlessness in face of enormous conflicts in which they feel no power to say 'yes' or 'no'. That many feel this cannot be denied. But we must surely add that in the West at least most people are far more protected against pain and disaster in their personal lives than at any time in history. We read in the papers of fearful catastrophes and monstrous acts: the shadows of Belsen and Dachau, Auschwitz, Dresden and Hiroshima lie over us from the near past, and of Vietnam and Biafra today. The scale has altered, and perhaps a quantitative change when sufficiently large does become qualitative. Technology has annihilated distance, so that we are aware, as past ages were not, of horrors taking place all over the world. But the history of mankind shows very few ages when there were not wars and disasters of the most hideous kind: terrible sieges, appalling sackings of cities, massacres, burnings alive, ghastly plagues and famines, without mentioning the horrors of childbirth, the gout and the stone, and of surgery, all borne with no alleviation. One sometimes wonders how many of the youthful audiences who watch these plays have ever themselves seen anyone die in agony or endured even the stopping of a tooth without an anaesthetic. Johnson thought the 'extrusion of *Gloucester's* eyes . . . too horrid to be endured in dramatick exhibition'; but he knew what physical pain was. I recently discovered to my surprise in questioning undergraduates that many of them did not feel the scene needed any justification. The obsession with violence and cruelty in what are the most prosperous areas of the world needs another explanation than the assumption that we live in worse times than our forefathers. 'The fish were small and bony, and the potatoes were a little burnt. We all acknowledged that we felt this something of a disappointment; but Mrs. Gummidge said she felt it more than we did, and shed tears again.'[1] It is the fact that we 'feel it more than they did' that requires explanation.

But the theatre of cruelty is less interesting than the theatre of what Lowell calls 'confusion'. Many people today, when they speak of 'the tragic', mean the arbitrarily terrible, something very near the 'absurd'. An American friend of mine, indignant at the many theories about the assassination of President Kennedy which postulated deliberate conspiracy and regarded the Warren report as an attempt to hush it all up, said to me that she thought that

[1] *David Copperfield*, Chap. III.

modern people shrank from the tragic: they had to find someone
to blame. They would not accept accident and rejected the idea
that an event of world-shaking importance could come about by
the act of a half-crazed, unstable creature who by a terrible chance
in a hundred happened to hit his mark. I was struck by this, and
said: 'Then it is pure accident that you feel to be the essence of
tragedy, crass casualty, or what Hardy called "Hap", not plot.'
She replied: 'Yes, I suppose I do. I think the tragic is the meaningless.'

There is a feeling today of the irrelevance to all our deepest
concerns of what is meant by 'plot', and a strong feeling also that
the dramatic falsifies reality rather than making it meaningful.
That entertaining undergraduate skit, *Rosencrantz and Guildenstern are Dead*, in its irreverent approach to a great tragic master-
piece, did not merely guy *Hamlet*. It guyed the whole idea of plot
and of the capacity of drama to present an acceptable illusion of
reality. What in Shakespeare's play makes in the end a pattern,
though it appears as random and accidental in the course of the
play, is here reduced back to the random. Picking up one of
Oscar Wilde's witticisms, and drawing heavily on Sartre and
Beckett, the author puts in the foreground the two spies summoned by Claudius to find out the cause of Hamlet's melancholy,
the 'baser natures' that came 'between the high and fell incensèd
points of mighty opposites'. Their incessant dialogue in an ante-
room is interrupted from time to time by incursions from the main
characters performing scraps of *Hamlet* which make no sense at
all. *En route* for Elsinore the two spies have fallen in with the
Players, who instruct them in the nature of dramatic illusion. In
their final encounter with the Players, who turn up on board the
ship which is bearing the two young men to their death in England,
and who emerge from barrels on the deck, like Jim Hawkins in
Treasure Island, they are presented with a last demonstration of
the actor's art. Declaring that death cannot be acted, Guildenstern stabs the Player King who 'dies in agony'. But he was
wounded with a trick dagger, the performance was a mere performance, and he gets up and obliges by deaths of all kinds. But

these are mere 'play-acting': 'Death is not anything . . . death is not. . . . It's the absence of presence, nothing more . . . the endless time of never coming back . . . a gap you can't see, and when the wind blows through it, it makes no sound. . . .' The author has taken from Shakespeare all the bafflement that *Hamlet* contains within its firm design, and also what is so constant in Shakespeare from the beginning: the sense of the limitations of art, the 'sacred discontent' of the great artist with the formulas and conventions of his art. Even though he must use them in his effort to display reality, he knows that there is 'that within which passes show'. When Richard II looks at himself in the glass and then casts the mirror to the ground with a theatrical gesture, he exclaims:

> *Mark, silent king, the moral of this sport—*
> *How soon my sorrow hath destroy'd my face.*

At which, Bolingbroke coldly observes: 'The shadow of your sorrow hath destroy'd the shadow of your face.' And Richard quickly agrees:

> *'Tis very true: my grief lies all within;*
> *And these external manner of laments*
> *Are merely shadows to the unseen grief*
> *That swells with silence in the tortur'd soul.*
> *There lies the substance.*

This 'substance' Shakespeare is always seeking to find 'shadows' for, aware that the persons of his plays are only as Puck calls them 'shadows' of human beings, and that, perhaps, human beings in the acts and words by which they present themselves to their fellows are only 'walking shadows' and 'poor players' strutting and fretting their hour upon the stage of life. But I am not convinced that attempts to present the 'substance' without employing the shadows bring us nearer to reality than Shakespeare's great shadow-plays do. Nor do attempts to present life as incoherent and inexplicable in works that mirror its incoherence arouse any very strong sense of mystery. Mystery is not the same as muddle. It is the understanding's acknowledgment of what is beyond understanding, which the understanding encounters in its effort to master its experience.

The reaction against plot and against dramatic expressiveness has obvious connections with changes in our conception of the nature of man, and the structure of personality. Actions interest us less than what lies behind them. We find their meaning not in conscious purpose or in their results, but in a complex of feelings and emotional attitudes to be uncovered in depths below conscious memory. These cannot be explored by willed introspection or the classic methods of self-examination. In vulgarized forms Freud's view of man can be used to provide glib explanations of all human conduct, reducing its variety and particularity to a limited number of stereotypes, and degrading all human achievements to the expression of animal and infantile urges. In itself, unvulgarized, the Freudian image of man is impressive and tragic, uncovering moral laws and moral tensions, and displaying the grandeur of human achievements within the limitations of human nature. It attempts to bring the immense forces of the irrational in man into the domain of reason, and, by teaching him to recognize the nature of the impulses that drive him, to teach him how he may master them, or at least live with them. But the stress of modern psychology has been away from a world of acts and consequences towards the contemplation of a world of dreams and fantasies, where the portentous and the terrible appear disguised as symbols often in themselves of the utmost triviality or of absurdity. Their import has to be interpreted before they have any import. Acts significant to the psychologist, such as habitually losing one's umbrella, are not in themselves imaginatively potent. They are made significant by what they point to, but in themselves, even after interpretation, they remain unimpressive. This revolution in thought has replaced such notions as crime or sin by the notion of sickness. The criminal, the sinner, the sick soul— this sequence has changed our whole attitude towards law and punishment. Punishment, it is held, may be inflicted for the sake of society, to deter men from crime or protect men from themselves, or it may be inflicted for the reform of the criminal. The concept of retribution, of retributive justice, has been deeply eroded. Yet the idea of retribution, though not, as some would make it, the sole element in the design of a tragedy, is still an essential element in great tragedies, as is the notion that men are responsible for what they do and must accept the consequences of their acts and the penalties they have incurred. The recognition that she is an offence and deserves punishment gives a dignity and grandeur to the Phaedra of Euripides and the Phèdre of Racine that the heroines of Tennessee Williams and other modern victims of Aphrodite lack. If, as we move from the world of Orestes to the world of Hamlet, we are conscious that we have moved from a world of crime and pollution to a world of sin and the dubieties of conscience, the world of Hamlet is still a world of crime and punishment, of acts that must meet their deserts, a world of guilt as well as a world of sorrow. When we come to *The Family Reunion* we are in a world where crime is of no interest, and sin is a sinful disposition arising from other sinful dispositions, a sickness of the soul that demands healing instead of punishment or penitence. A sense of the tragic as a universal sickness can produce works of almost unbearable pathos. But unrelieved pathos is monotonous. If excessive calls are made on pity its springs soon run dry. And if pity is akin to love, it is also dangerously near contempt. The only comment on plays concerned with the 'human predicament' is either a patronizing one, 'Poor things!'; or perhaps a mood of self-pity in which we think we are all 'poor things'. *The Family Reunion* avoids this. There is little pathos; but there is also little awe. Its greatness lies in the poetry by which it explores states of mind. The characters lack imaginative body. Harry inspires neither pity nor fear. At times he arouses irritation, and even boredom, the kind of irritation we feel with those who are much preoccupied with their own inner lives or are under analysis and cannot talk of anything else. It is possible to see why Eliot turned from the attempt to write a modern tragedy to modern comedy. Though drawing-room comedy and Wildean farce provided weak models or formulas, they were still formulas of some dramatic vitality. No formulas existed in which he could embody his modern sense of 'the tragic', and *The Family Reunion* teases us by its attempt to embody an essentially undramatic conception in dramatic form. Eliot's sense of the tragic is found in his poetry, in *The Waste Land*, in *The Hollow Men*, in many of the speeches in *The Family Reunion*, and in *East Coker*. In this last poem he broke away from the traditional concepts and the traditional language of Christian theology and Christian poetry to render his sense of the incoherence and inconclusiveness of our experience and our achievements, the complication of the pattern of dead and living. Christ appears not in such traditional images as the Lamb that was slain, or the High Priest making offering for the sins of the world, but as the 'wounded surgeon', probing with his steel the distempered part, and, in his own and our pain, 'resolving the enigma of the fever chart'. *East Coker* is about 'the dark', about waiting, about loneliness, and declares, perhaps prophetically, that 'to be restored our sickness must grow worse'. It is a tragic poem in the modern sense of the tragic, not least in its open and unconcluded end: 'We must be still and still moving.'

When I attempted to suggest a connection between the religious temper of the later Middle Ages and the emergence of tragedy in Elizabethan England, referring to the Anselmian doctrine of the Atonement, the conception of the Mass as the Holy Sacrifice, the obsession with sin and penance, and the growth of the conception of tragedy as showing less the arbitrariness of Fortune and more the just judgments of God on sin, I was speaking of a temper and an emphasis that is often regarded as 'orthodox', but which is, in fact, a late medieval orthodoxy. Other conceptions have been dominant at different times and in different places. When Archbishop Cranmer composed his Order for Holy Communion he supplied what we do not find in earlier liturgies, a General Confession followed by an Absolution and by 'Comfortable Words'. The passionate language of that General Confession, which far exceeds the language of the General Confession he wrote for Matins and Evensong, expresses in hauntingly rhythmic phrases the sense of the burden of guilt as 'intolerable'. The great prayer that was added to the Prayer Book of 1662 is Bishop Reynolds's

General Thanksgiving. To turn from one to the other is to move out of darkness into sunshine; but I do not know by what criterion either is to be regarded as more religious or more Christian than the other. In the recent liturgical reform Cranmer's General Confession has gone and a much less extravagant expression of penitence has been substituted. Liturgies are notoriously very conservative; but it has at last been realized that it is impossible, as it has been for a very long time, for congregations to use language so remote from anything they truly feel. We are accustomed to be told that the Mass is a great drama. All liturgies are dramatic in the sense that in them things are done. But anyone familiar with both knows that there is a great difference between the Roman Mass, and Liturgies dependent upon it, and the Holy Orthodox Liturgy. The one has climax and point: everything moves to a supreme moment. The Orthodox Liturgy seems pointless to someone brought up in the Western tradition. The sense of the human taken up into the divine, and the divine descending into the human is diffused, not concentrated. It seems undramatic, concerned with intersections of the timeless and time. It is less a Holy Sacrifice; more a Eucharist. Liturgical reforms in the West seem to be moving towards this and away from the drama of the sacring bell and the Elevation. Again, the crucifix, which many think of as the prime Christian symbol, has not been the prime symbol always and everywhere. In the catacombs and on early Christian sarcophagi there are other symbols: the good shepherd, the philosopher or wise man. Ravenna can show us a Christ of the Legions, a common soldier treading on the lion and the basilisk; and it was Christ reigning in power, the beardless Christ of San Vitale or the bearded Syrian Christ as Pantocrator that earlier ages set before men rather than the suffering Christ upon the Cross. The Romanesque portal that shows monsters and strange beasts entwined and menacing on pillars and arches, surrounding a Christ serenely reigning in the centre is more congenial to modern religious feeling than the Gothic images of the suffering Christ and the Christ of Judgment.

To sum up, I believe that conditions today are not conducive to the creation of tragedy, and that the modern sense of the tragic does not, and cannot find expression in works that can truly or fruitfully be compared with Greek or Shakespearian tragedies. It is only in rare periods that men are able to produce great works of art which present an image of human life in which order and design can embrace those elements of experience that most call in question the desire to find order and design in life; and which, with the ambiguity of great works of art, allow of different readings of the image they present as 'what must be' and as the protest 'must it be?'. In these works the greatness of men is seen in their acceptance of responsibility for what they do. The world is a field of moral values where, although virtue and innocence bring no safety, wrong meets with retribution. Such a vision is not unconsonant with the Christian vision of man's lot on earth; indeed, of all the highly-developed religions, Christianity, in its declaration that all our earthly experience is meaningful however mysterious it seems in our experience of it, most directs the imagination towards the contemplation of the course of things in this world. Tragedy appeared in ancient Greece and Christian Europe at a time when the thought of divine power and divine judgment appear the dominant religious conceptions, and the sense of guilt the most oppressive burden on the religious consciousness. But it appears also in ages confident in man's power to explore the world and in exploring understand it.

We live today in the still unresolved religious, moral and political crisis of the nineteenth century, in a climate of uncertainty in the formulations of religious beliefs and of ethical standards, and in a world where the immense extensions of knowledge in every sphere have made a synthesis of our knowledge into anything that could be called a 'world view' impossible. However much the 'world views' or 'world pictures' that have been constructed for earlier ages simplify what men actually thought and felt, it is difficult to believe that any future scholars will ever attempt to construct such a systematic picture of common beliefs and assumptions for the twentieth century. If they attempt to characterize our age at all, no doubt it will be under the metaphor of a 'climate' rather than a 'picture'. W. H. Auden called his long modern poem 'The Age of Anxiety'. The same term has been employed to describe the centuries in which Christianity was born and established itself. The Christian revelation met, and in meeting absorbed and was absorbed into the anxieties, the distresses, the knowledge, the wisdom and the insights of a world in which men's hearts were failing them for fear. We have much more in common with the temper of that world of late antiquity, demon-ridden, given over to the search for a way of life in esoteric cults and magic practices, politically insecure, and artistically decadent, than we have with the temper of fifth-century Athens or Elizabethan England. It was a world looking for release from its fears, for grounds of hope, and for a renewal of the springs of human energy and enterprise. Eliot's original title for *Murder in the Cathedral* was 'Fear in the Way'. Salvation today means more release from fear than release from guilt.

I would like to end with a postscript. We inevitably find in great works of past ages what speaks to our condition, embodies our own fears and anxieties and confirms our own assurances and values, or our lack of assurance and value. But relevance, like happiness, or health, eludes those who deliberately seek for it. Because our age is peculiarly aware of the irrational, of the incoherence of our lives, sees sin as sickness rather than the willed choice of wrong, and is unsympathetic to the idea of the heroic, our response to Shakespearian Tragedy is different from the response of Johnson or of Coleridge or of Bradley. Elements of which they were aware, but which to them were minor elements in the whole, bulk larger to us. But the deliberate attempt to make these great works illustrative of our own condition, so that they do not quarrel with our conceptions is an appalling impoverishment of what they have to give us. We rightly object to the Christian, the Marxist, or the Freudian who reduces works of imagination and power to exemplifications of the doctrines he holds. We should equally protest against 'Shakespeare our Contemporary', and the fashionable attempt to present Shakespeare as an existentialist. To make the tragedies of Shakespeare conform to our idea of 'the tragic' as 'the meaningless', to sacrifice Shake-speare the poet to our desire for spectacle and violence, is out-rageous arrogance. A false concept of progress is at work here, which imprisons us in the contemporary, in our own anxieties and problems. The humble and reverent contemplation of great works of the past can release us from the prison of present fears and anxieties and, in so releasing us, give us new understanding of them.

RELIGIOUS POETRY

The Ewing Lectures

Delivered at the University of California
at Los Angeles, March 1966

I

Religious Poetry: a Definition

The topic I have chosen for these lectures is one that has been in my mind for some time. I have been engaged on and off, in thinking about compiling and editing a 'Book of Religious Verse'. The task has led me to ponder problems of definition, arrangement and presentation, as well as the obvious problems of selection. It was T. S. Eliot who asked me to undertake this book. If anyone else had, I think I should possibly have refused, doubting the value of such an anthology for critics and scholars, and even for that ill-defined character the general reader. But some correspondence with Mr. Eliot cleared my scruples and forced me to examine the case for regarding religious poetry as a special category of poetry and the benefits of so regarding it. This led me to ask myself certain questions and to examine certain critical statements and critical presumptions.

The first question was whether there is a definite and definable department of poetry that can be categorized as 'religious poetry'; if so, and common usage suggests that there is, what are its limits? How do we define a religious poem? After we have made our definition, does the poetry we decide to call religious poetry present peculiar problems to the critical reader that are different from the problems that poetry in general presents? Do we find ourselves applying, or ought we to apply, special criteria of judgment in considering religious poetry? To put it another way, are there special pleasures and special interests that religious poetry presents; or, on the contrary, are there limitations and restrictions on the religious poet that make religious poetry a species of 'minor poetry'. Is the religious poet something less than 'a man speaking to men'? Does he, as a sympathetic reviewer of Theodore Roethke's last volume in the *TLS* said, speak with 'the authority of religion' and not with 'the human authority of poetry'? If this is so, is it because there is some fundamental difference between the religious approach to experience and the poet's which inhibits the religious poet from achieving the full power of poetry? Or is it, on the contrary, because the religious experience and the poetic are too close to each other? Is the substance of religion in itself too poetical to be transmuted into poetry? Is the poet defeated because his work of ordering and interpreting his experience and rendering it in moving and expressive symbols has been done for him by generations of men, who have found and established symbols more powerful and expressive than any he could discover for himself? Is the religious poet inevitably a 'minor poet', because more than half his work has been done for him? Is he debarred from being either a seer or a true maker and condemned to be merely a versifier of conceptions that are not his own? To answer questions of this kind requires an attempt to define religion and to consider assumptions about the nature of poetry and the poet's function and task. But neither the concept of religion nor the concept of poetry is a stable one through the centuries. And it is precisely here, I think, that the interest and value of studying 'religious poetry' as a genre lies: in the variations from age to age in the concept of religion and the concept of poetry and the interactions between them.

A dislike or at any rate a distaste for religious poetry is by no means confined to those unsympathetic to religion. On the contrary, the classic expression of such distaste comes from Dr. Johnson, the most devout of all great critics; it was T. S. Eliot who was willing to allow that religious poetry was 'a variety of *minor* poetry'; and it was Lord David Cecil, introducing the *Oxford Book of Christian Verse,* who declared that in 'Christian Europe' religious emotion 'has not proved the most fertile soil for poetry'. Each of these critics gives different reasons for his reservations over religious poetry; and each expresses or implies a different theory of poetry in suggesting why religious poetry does not provide, or only rarely provides, the full pleasures of poetry. Johnson's attack on 'poetical devotion', which occurs in his *Life of Waller*, is the fullest and most carefully reasoned expression of the view that there is an incompatibility between worship and prayer, that is religious activity, and poetry. It must be recognized that what Johnson is attacking is 'poetical devotion'. He carefully excludes didactic poetry, in which the doctrines of religion are defended, from his discussion; since 'he who has the happy power of arguing in verse, will not lose it because his subject is sacred'. He also excludes poetry in praise of the creation, in which 'the subject of the disputation is not piety, but the motives to piety; that of the description is not God, but the works of God'. It is 'contemplative piety', or 'the intercourse between God and the human soul' that he roundly declares 'cannot be poetical'; since 'man admitted to implore the mercy of his Creator, and plead the merits of his Redeemer, is already in a higher state than poetry can confer'. Johnson held that the essence of poetry was 'invention' and novelty he thought out of place in religion. Poetry, he held, pleases 'by exhibiting an idea more grateful to the mind than things themselves afford'; but this delightful feigning is out of place in religion which 'must be shewn as it is; suppression and addition equally corrupt it'. From poetry, Johnson declares, 'the reader justly expects, and from good poetry always obtains, the enlargement of his comprehension and elevation of his fancy; but this is rarely to be hoped by Christians from metrical devotion. . . . Omnipotence cannot be exalted; Infinity cannot be amplified; Perfection cannot be improved'. And if we turn from the object of worship to the worshipper, we are in no better case: 'Faith, invariably uniform, cannot be invested by fancy with decorations. Thanksgiving . . . is to be felt rather than expressed. Repentance, trembling in the presence of the Judge, is not at leisure for cadences and epithets. Supplication of man to man may diffuse itself through many topicks of persuasion; but supplication to God can only cry for mercy.' Summing up, Johnson states firmly that in religious poetry 'Poetry loses its lustre and its power,

[*123*]

because it is applied to the decoration of something more excellent than itself. All that pious verse can do is to help the memory, and delight the ear . . .; it supplies nothing to the mind. The ideas of Christian Theology are too simple for eloquence, too sacred for fiction, and too majestick for ornament.' Johnson is equating religion with the practice of religion, and of the Christian religion at that, regarding its doctrines as presented to the human mind for reverent contemplation and understanding, bringing with them the obligation to worship, prayer and moral effort. Poetry was, on his theory, 'the art of uniting pleasure with truth by calling imagination to the aid of reason'. In the sphere of religion the imagination was an intruder, as was all rhetoric and eloquence.

T. S. Eliot was less severe on 'poetical devotion', or what he called 'devotional poetry'.[1] He does not deny that it may be genuine poetry of a high order; but he thinks it is of 'a special kind'. He declares that 'for the great majority of people who love poetry, "*religious* poetry" is a variety of *minor* poetry: the religious poet is not a poet who is treating the whole subject matter of poetry in a religious spirit, but a poet who is dealing with a con-fined part of this subject matter: who is leaving out what men consider their major passions, and thereby confessing his ignor-ance of them.' Adding that he thinks this is 'the real attitude of most poetry lovers towards such poets as Vaughan, or Southwell, or Crashaw, or George Herbert, or Gerard Hopkins', he is 'ready to admit that up to a point these critics are right':

> For there is a kind of poetry, such as most of the work of the authors I have mentioned, which is the product of a special religious awareness, which may exist without the general aware-ness which we expect of the major poet. In some poets, or in some of their works, this general awareness may have existed; but the preliminary steps which represent it may have been suppressed, and only the end-product presented. Between these, and those in which the religious or devotional genius repre-sents the *special* and limited awareness, it may be very difficult to discriminate. I do not pretend to offer Vaughan, or South-

[1] See the essay on 'Religion and Literature', *Essays Ancient and Modern* (1936), pp. 93–112.

well, or George Herbert, or Hopkins as major poets: I feel sure
that the first three, at least, are poets of this limited awareness.
They are not great religious poets in the sense in which Dante,
or Corneille, or Racine, even in those of their plays which do not
touch upon Christian themes, are great Christian religious poets.
Or even in the sense in which Villon and Baudelaire, with all their
imperfections and delinquencies, are Christian poets.

This clearly is a very different view from Johnson's. Eliot does
not feel an incompatibility between the practice of religion and
the writing of poetry, and does not deny that in its limited way
poetical devotion can please. We have moved from the conception of the poet as maker and artist, adorning his chosen subject
by imagination and eloquence, to a different conception of poetry
and the poet. The poet is not distinguished from other men by
his capacity for 'invention' but by his 'awareness'. He is a more
sensitive being than ordinary men, more 'aware' of his experience.
And on the grounds that we can distinguish the major from the
minor poet by the greater width and depth of his 'awareness',
Eliot finds the religious poet too limited in his range, too sensitively aware of his relation to God to be sensitively aware of his
relation to his fellows, or to nature, or the hundred and one other
occupations of men when they are not upon their knees. But having done so, Eliot very characteristically confuses the whole
issue by suggesting a quite different conception of 'religious
poetry', as poetry in which the whole of life is treated in a religious
spirit. Like Johnson, he equates religion with Christianity, and
finds the 'great religious poets', that is Christian poets, to be
Dante, Corneille and Racine, and, although he plainly feels there
is a further distinction to be made, Villon and Baudelaire. This
opens the gates very wide, and suggests an even wider opening
if we are willing to allow that religion and Christianity are not
interchangeable terms.

Yet another point of view was expressed by Lord David Cecil,
who was commissioned by the Oxford University Press in 1940 to
produce an *Oxford Book of Christian Verse*. Lord David rightly
respected the terms of his commission, and 'among poems of

equal literary merit' by an author chose those poems that 'seemed most significant of Christian feeling'. With the exception of Blake, he confined his selection to writers whose 'poems are consistent with the doctrines of orthodox Christianity'. His principles were sound and his choice excellent. But, on those principles, many of our greatest poets were totally unrepresented, and others, such as Wordsworth, were not represented by their greatest poems. In his preface Lord David made some suggestions as to why this was so. 'Religious emotion', he declared, 'is the most sublime known to man. But, in Christian Europe at any rate, it has not proved the most fertile soil for poetry. Though the great religious poets have been equal to any, they have been fewer in number than the great secular poets. And a large proportion of religious verse is poor stuff. The average hymn is a by-word for forced feeble sentiment, flat conventional expression. And those poets who have invoked both the sacred and the profane muse have, with some striking exceptions, found themselves more comfortable with the profane.' Lord David goes on to try to find, as Johnson did, an explanation for what both complain of, the feebleness of much religious verse. At first they seem to be agreed, when Lord David begins by stating, 'The very loftiness of the religious sentiment is in part responsible.' But then they diverge. To Johnson the strength and purity of religious feeling was what made any attempt to poeticize it improper and doomed to defeat. But to Lord David the opposite is the reason.

A writer's best poetry is usually the expression of his keenest feeling. And though many people have caught a passing whiff of pious emotion, only a few have felt it with the strength and the continuity that they feel sexual love or pleasure in nature. The faintness of their experience reflects itself in the verses in which they seek to communicate it. Further, those in whom the emotion is strong do not always have the faculty to express it. Rarely, indeed, does humanity produce a Blake gifted with the power to forge new and living symbols for the cosmic mysteries of spiritual experience. Most poets fall back on the traditional symbols of the orthodox liturgy. And these, though magnificently impressive on the lips of their creators, tend to lose their vitality on those of others. It is the poet's essential quality that he speaks with his own voice.

Lord David goes on to say that the Christian poet is faced with special difficulties, for 'poetry should be the spontaneous expression of the spirit; the poet lets his personality burst forth without concealment; but 'the devout person feels it profane to show himself in all his earthy imperfections. . . . He will allow himself to express only unexceptionable sentiments, love, reverence, humility: will voice no aspiration save for a purer soul and stronger faith. As for using any but the most decorous language to express his feelings, the very idea horrifies him. . . . The writer, that is, does not say what he really feels, but what he thinks he ought to feel: and he speaks not in his own voice but in the solemn tones that seem fitting to his solemn subject.'

A good many of these statements seem questionable. To begin with, it is no doubt perfectly true that profound and strong religious emotion does not necessarily go with great poetic gifts; but it is equally true that other profound and strong emotions may be felt by persons without the gift for expressing them. We cannot assume that the best love poets were the best lovers; and there must be many persons capable of passionate and exalted love who either could not, or in most cases had not the slightest desire to, write poetry about their feelings. There does not seem any particular reason why we should assume that there are more inarticulate and poetically inept persons among those with whom religion is a powerful emotion than among those who feel other emotions strongly. As questionable is the remark that 'though many people have felt a passing whiff of pious emotion, only a few have felt it with the strength and continuity that they feel sexual love or pleasure in nature.' Is religion really so weak a rival to sexual love? History records countless persons who have died for their religion; martyrs of love, though more popular as subjects for drama and fiction, are less common in life. But leaving on one side sexual love—for it is the mode today to assume that we all are, or should be, great lovers—is pleasure in nature a profound emotion to large numbers of people? I should have thought that the number of people capable of intense and sustained rather than mild and occasional pleasure in nature—as far as such things can be measured statistically—was far fewer than the number of those to whom religion is an intense and permanent emotional experience. Lord David's theory of poetry is different from Johnson's or Eliot's. The poet, for him, is not distinguished from other men by his capacity for invention or by his awareness, but by his strength of feeling. Poetry is the spontaneous expression of the poet's feelings and should reveal the writer's personality without concealment; it should show the man without a mask. This theory that poetry is the expression of personality and that its essence is spontaneity provides an explanation of the special difficulties of the religious poet rather different from Johnson's: that the Christian poet 'does not say what he really feels, but what he thinks he ought to feel': and is afraid of using any but the most decorous language.

On these last two points C. S. Lewis challenged Lord David in a review of his anthology,[1] pointing out that, on the contrary, much devotional poetry had as its subject not what the poet ought to feel but the fact that he did not feel as he ought. As Lewis wittily observed, most love poetry seems to suggest that the lover is always at the highest pitch of feeling. The moments when he is bored with his lady, or critical of her, or just out of sorts, or out of temper, or out of love are rarely commemorated by love poets. The religious poets show much more awareness of the vicissitudes of their emotional lives, and are much more ready to treat of their failures and perplexities. Further, Lewis pointed out that, far from being over-decorous, religious poets are commonly very bold in the images they employ and the language they use about the Deity, echoing here the language of Scripture which is by no means remarkable for primness and decorum. Finally, Lewis challenged the idea that there is more feeble religious poetry than feeble poetry on other subjects, and asked whether, if the badness of hymns is a by-word, we can place against them any successful commissioned or public poems in modern times. The modern

[1] *Review of English Studies* (January 1941).

hymn is no worse and no better than the modern patriotic poem. Lewis was a very able and acute controversialist, and he put his finger on weaknesses in Lord David's arguments. All the same he did not dispose of the fact that Lord David started from: that in any anthology of Christian verse we shall find, after the seventeenth century, that our greatest poets are not represented, or are represented by their weaker poems. And, although there are religious poems of great beauty and interest which we can have no hesitation in regarding as fine poems, there are also a great many in which 'the piety is more remarkable than the poetry', which are at best only faintly interesting. Is this because of a decline in the strength of religious belief, or of changes in religious concepts and alterations of emphasis, or is it because of changes in the concepts of poetry and of the poet's function? Johnson felt, as apparently Southwell and Donne and Herbert did not, that poetry, the art of fiction, could only degrade religion, which is concerned with truth. Lord David feels that poetry, the expression of spontaneous and profound personal feeling, is inhibited by religion, because all religions, not merely the Christian religion, declare 'le moi est haïssable', and demand from us some attempt to deny or transcend the self. Religious poetry is distasteful to Johnson because either it attempts an inappropriate originality and eloquence where these things are not required or, if it uses the proper language of devotion, it perforce falls short of poetry. To Lord David it is only rarely successful because, except on rare occasions, it lacks originality, the poet expressing what he ought to feel as a Christian rather than what he himself, as an individual, feels.

Lord David was commissioned to produce a *Book of Christian Verse*. There is no *Oxford Book of Religious Verse*: but there is a volume called *The Oxford Book of Mystical Verse*, first published in 1917 and still in print. (It has been reprinted ten times, the last printing being in 1953.) The editors, D. H. S. Nicholson and A. E. H. Lee, selected from all centuries beginning with the thirteenth. But, of their six-hundred-and-odd pages, only a hundred are devoted to poems written before the year 1800. This volume contains more feeble poetry than any I know, except *The*

Stuffed Owl, and makes almost any hymn-book seem a collection of classic masterpieces. The personality that Lord David feels to be inhibited by the restraints of orthodox Christian thought and tradition here bursts forth unimpeded, and the results of this liberation are most dismal and tedious. There is an overwhelming impression of solemn egoism, of 'windy suspiration of forced breath', of loose, lolloping metres, of poems that begin from nowhere and go on to nowhere—all one insufferable middle—or of little pieces of religious fancy unchecked by decorum or the rigours of a dogmatic system. The word 'mystical' is a fatal word. It took on a new life in the late nineteenth century, and from having been a term of abuse became a term of praise. It is perhaps unfair to pillory this book, which is beginning to have the fascination of a historical monument, like the last hundred pages of the *Oxford Book of English Verse*, with which it should be compared. It represents a moment in the history of taste and of thought when it was held that personal experience was the only proper subject of true poetry, and that religion meant personal religious experience, interpreted as emotional experience.

A different mood is represented by the *Penguin Book of Religious Verse*, edited by R. S. Thomas in 1963. Mr. Thomas, who is a priest of the Church in Wales, is himself a poet of distinction and refinement, in the honourable tradition of parson-poets. He was awarded the Queen's Medal for Poetry in 1965. In his anthology he abandons chronology and arranges his poems under themes. His aim is to display five aspects of religion imaginatively presented in poetry; and religion he defines as an experience of ultimate reality. This is not an anthology of Christian verse and Mr. Thomas has 'attempted to broaden the meaning of the term "religious" to accommodate twentieth-century sensibility.' His emphasis, he insists, has been on the quality of the poetry. All anthologists, one may assume, believe that their emphasis is on quality, that the poems they have chosen are good poems. But there is a peculiar difficulty in applying the test of quality to religious poetry; and this remains whether we define religion narrowly or broadly. It is extremely difficult to disentangle religious and aesthetic responses. If we take religious poetry in the narrow sense as the poetry of Christian devotion, many poems, particularly hymns, have been so familiar to us from childhood and are so involved with our continuing acceptance, or our rejection, of the religion we were brought up in that it is impossible to see them as aesthetic objects. With hymns there is the obstacle of the tunes they are wedded to in memory, as well as the personal memories with which they are entangled. Is it possible to consider 'Abide with me' or 'Lead kindly light' as religious poems apart from the rather sickening melodies to which they are sung, and memories of Sunday evenings and funerals, not to mention the popularity of 'Abide with me' at Cup Finals? I feel incapable of deciding how good or bad as poetry many hymns are. They are so intricately involved with my life that I cannot criticize or evaluate them. Their poetic quality seems as irrelevant as the question whether one's mother is beautiful. They have gathered a value from experience which has destroyed whatever quality they have as poetry. Those who have revolted against the religion in which they were brought up are not in any better case. They are probably as blind to what merits familiar hymns have as I am to their defects. If, on the other hand, we give religious poetry a wider connotation, as Messrs. Nicholson and Lee did, and as Mr. Thomas more daringly does, approval of the views, sympathy with the experience or aspirations expressed, is likely to blur aesthetic judgment just as seriously. If our test of a good religious poem is that is seems to us to enshrine an experience we regard as genuinely religious, we are in danger of valuing the poem because we value the experience, irrespective of the power or lack of power with which it is expressed. As the moralistic critic is so obsessed with morality that he values works of art primarily on the grounds of their moral usefulness or moral danger, so the critic of religious poetry, attempting to escape from the shackles of the Christian tradition and move out into the wider area of religious experience, is tempted to find merit in what echoes his own preoccupations and seems to him to present a valuable and truly religious attitude or experience.

Mr. Thomas has not wholly escaped this danger. He groups his poems under five headings: consciousness of God, of the self, of negation, of the impersonal or unnameable, and of completion: God, Self, Nothing, It, All. The first poem in the section 'God' is by Byron, and is called 'The Prayer of Nature'. It begins:

> *Father of Lights! great God of Heaven!*
> *Hear'st thou the accents of despair?*
> *Can guilt like man's be e'er forgiven?*
> *Can vice atone for crimes by prayer?*

This is, obviously, an anthology of the 'Age of Anxiety', when *'angst'* is regarded as the basic religious emotion and despair is held to be a more vivid and profound experience than faith and hope. It is sly and amusing of Mr. Thomas to place next to this gloomy piece by Byron a hymn of Addison's which begins:

> *When all thy mercies, O my God,*
> *My rising soul surveys,*
> *Transported with the view, I'm lost*
> *In wonder, love and praise.*

The juxtaposition of Byron and Addison is entertaining and thought-provoking; but the test of quality seems to have yielded to the desire to set *angst* against complacency and perhaps to reveal Byron as, if not the more truly religious spirit, a spirit more attuned to contemporary sensibility. The feeble rhetoric of Byron —questions expecting the answer 'No'—and the monotonous inversions of Addison are in the style of the worst hymns. Neither poem is worth its place in an anthology of only a hundred and eighty pages, except as an example of religious sentiment. Mr. Thomas's anthology is of the greatest interest to anyone wishing to understand the religious climate of today, not least because it is a collection made by a parson. Since I have criticized some of his inclusions, I must add that it contains some magnificent poetry, much of it not well known. But it is of less interest to a student of poetry. It gives the reader no opportunity to make fruitful comparisons of his own between the poems collected under Mr.

Thomas's five headings and arbitrarily juxtaposed. It is stated in the introduction that the publishers felt that a chronological sequence 'can militate against effective juxtaposition of different authors or passages': but 'effective juxtaposition' by an anthologist, by over-directing the reader's attention to certain points of likeness or difference, inhibits him from finding others. More serious is the vagueness of the concept 'religious sensibility' as a basis for choice. It is even vaguer than 'religious emotion', and does not provide a sufficiently firm delimitation of the subject-matter of the poems assembled for comparison. We need to establish a criterion of 'likeness' before we can discuss 'unlikeness'.

For the purposes of criticism or scholarship (or the making of anthologies) definitions need to be strict. Under the head of 'Nothing' Mr. Thomas includes passages from Byron's *Manfred* and *Cain*, from *Measure for Measure* and *Macbeth*. When we have said that Byron has no gift for writing in blank verse, and added that his schoolboy atheism cannot stand comparison with the seriousness of the terrible passage from *Measure for Measure* in which Shakespeare makes only too vividly apprehensible to the imagination the horror of the fear of death, or with Macbeth's sense of the utter meaninglessness of human life, we have said all that there is to say. Further, is this shudder of the mind and nerves at the thought of non-being, or at the thought of idiotic meaninglessness, serious, terrible and profound as such an experience may be, and in Shakespeare's rendering imaginatively is, to be called religious, without destroying the meaning of words? There is surely a real difference between the cry 'Ay, but to die, and go we know not where; To lie in cold obstruction and to rot', or Hardy's poignant poem 'Afterwards', or Housman's sombre and stoical 'Be still, my soul, be still; the arms you bear are brittle', as expressions of 'Nothing', and the 'terrible sonnets' of Hopkins, 'No worst, there is none', and 'I wake and feel the fell of dark, not day', which makes it possible to distinguish these last two poems as religious poems and say that the others are not, using 'religious' not as a term of praise or blame but as a defining term. And when we have done so, fruitful comparisons at once leap to the mind—

with the Holy Sonnets of Donne, with some of the poems of dereliction in Herbert's *The Temple*, 'Denial' for instance, or with Cowper's 'The Castaway'. If we narrow our field and interpret 'religious' strictly, we can make genuine comparisons between the sensibilities and modes of expression of different men and different ages. If we accept that 'modern sensibility' has come to feel that 'wherever and whenever man broods upon himself and his destiny, he does it as a spiritual and self-conscious being without peer in the universe which we know' and that the expression of such brooding in verse is religious poetry, we have disposed pretty completely of Mr. Eliot's view that religious poetry is a kind of minor poetry, but at the cost of making the term so wide as to be meaningless. Coleridge's 'Dejection' and Wordsworth's 'Ode on Intimations of Immortality' are not religious poems in any exact sense of the term. If we wish to categorize them, we might call them 'meditative poems' or 'philosophic poems'; though as soon as we do so, it is plain that they are not to be categorized. Profoundly moving, deeply beautiful, and illuminating as they are, they are not written out of that sense of commitment and obligation which is the essence of religion.

Religion is more than attitudes, aspirations, emotions, speculations and intimations. Although it can include all these things, it includes them within a way of life consciously accepted in obedience to what are felt to be imperatives from without the self that are binding. It expresses itself, and has throughout all ages and in all societies, in rituals that have to be performed and in rules of conduct that are obligatory both personally and socially. As Blake declared, and modern sociologists would seem to agree, 'there is no natural religion'. Religion is, or appears to be to those who accept it, revelation, something not invented but given, or handed down from those to whom it has been given. Such revelation offers itself, to be accepted with awe, thanksgiving and worship; to be acknowledged as making claims and passing judgments, and consequently demanding of man the response of prayer and penitence. The peculiar interest and the peculiar beauty of religious poetry lies precisely in the fact that the poet who writes as a religious man does write in fetters. He writes as a man committed and his commitment, even if it is not stated, is implied. Whether he attempts to render in his own words and images the substance of the revelation received, or to render his response to it, he asks the reader to accept, at least during the reading of the poem, truths which are not presented as personal discoveries, values that are not his individual values, and to measure the experiences treated against standards that the poem itself does not create but whose existence it takes for granted. To define religious poetry as poetry that treats of revelation and of man's response to revelation does not equate religious poetry with Christian poetry; but the great majority of English religious poems on this definition will be found to be Christian poems in some sense. Since 'No' is a response as well as 'Yes', we can include as religious poems some poems in which the response is rejection of the Christian revelation and doubt of its truth, as well as poems of mockery and satire on the pretensions of the religious. There are also a good many poems, mainly written in the later centuries, which are clearly religious in this sense but are not Christian, such as Shelley's 'Hymn to Intellectual Beauty'. This, unlike Wordsworth's great Ode, does not touch on Platonic doctrine to illuminate speculation on human life but makes of Platonism a religion. It expresses with burning faith the religious sense of the absolute demand of revelation upon the soul and conscience. And, equally, we should include many passages from *The Prelude* in which Wordsworth gives sublime expression to his sense of revelation and of dedication.

Since revelation is of necessity made in place and time, and since all that is received can only be received according to the capacity of the receiver, the substance of what is claimed to be, or is presented as, eternal truth is intricately entwined with the accidents of time and place and human personality. We may come nearer recognizing the substance if we accept our limitations as historic beings and concentrate on the accidents; and have a more acute sense of the sameness of human experiences by stressing difference than by too hastily asserting likeness. A chronological

and historical approach, which sets the religious poet in the context of the thought and the poetry of his own age, displaying the
interaction of religious and aesthetic ideals, goes some way to
answering the question Lord David raised and which troubled
Mr. Thomas. For one reason why Mr. Thomas spread his net so
wide was that he felt distress at including so little great poetry in
an anthology of religious verse. If we look at religious poetry
through the centuries, and see it changing with changes in Christian
thought and experience, reflecting not only the personal circumstances and personal experiences of the author but also changing
relations between religion and secular thought, and affected by
changing concepts of the nature of poetry and the arts, and by
changing fashions in poetry and by dominant modes in secular
poetry, we can see that certain ages provide, in Eliot's words,
'conditions that seem unpropitious'. How far this is because they
are less religious than other ages is not a question a literary critic
can answer—or anyone else for that matter until, if the day ever
comes, the Day of Judgment. It would be rash to assume that outside Scotland in the eighteenth century men and women had
ceased to fall in love, or felt only tepid affection for each other,
because Burns is the only considerable love poet in a hundred
years. Nor would it be safe to assume from the prevalence of
satire in the period from 1660 to 1740 that men and women in this
period were exceptionally worldly, corrupt, venal and foolish,
and poets exceptionally morally sensitive and high-minded. Propitious ages for the writing of religious verse, as far as a literary
historian can judge, would seem to be ages in which poetry is
regarded as an art, and the poet is not thought to be betraying his
vocation as a poet by writing what is not unlike a commissioned
work, a work in which he devotes his skill to the expression of
what are accepted as known truths. Less propitious ages are those
in which originality is demanded of the poet—he is not expected
to make more vivid to us what we already know and feel, but to
makes us know and feel what without him we should have never
known or felt—and in which we apply the test of whether the
poet sincerely feels what in the poem he presents himself as feel-

ing. If it is the test of originality that we apply, if we demand fresh personal experience spontaneously felt and expressed with the appearance of spontaneity, then religion will be felt to inhibit poetry, or religious sentiment will take the place of religion as a subject for poetry. If we demand the accent of sincerity, we may feel with Johnson that the art of poetry is incompatible with deep religious feeling. By the same test he dismissed *Lycidas*. It did not for him have the accent of true grief: 'passion runs not after remote allusions and obscure opinions'—'where there is leisure for fiction, there is little grief.' It was distressing to him that poets should mingle 'trifling fictions' with 'awful and sacred truths'. Propitious ages are those in which the poet can rely on his readers doing much of his work for him, seeing implications and accepting standards that the poem does not itself make and create. Less propitious ages are those in which a poem is expected to make its own field of reference, in which the poet has to convince us of the importance of what he has to say, and must prove his credentials not merely as a poet but as a religious man, and must also prove, in some measure, the credentials of religion.

These last are, I suppose, the conditions to which Eliot was referring in *East Coker*. The religious poet today has to meet a problem of communication that did not exist for earlier centuries. Words and symbols that lay to hand for earlier writers as sure to evoke a universal response have lost their power. The effect of the disappearance of a general acceptance of Christianity, however conventional, half-hearted, or even cynical it may have been with many people, can be seen in the two most impressive religious poets of the nineteenth and twentieth centuries. In Hopkins and Eliot there is a certain straining of feeling and language that one is not aware of in poets of earlier ages. In Hopkins, this takes the form of an eccentric violence; in Eliot of a cryptic obscurity. It is as if the one were saying 'Listen, you *must* believe me; I really do feel this most intensely'; and the other, 'Guess what I *really* mean —see how far you can go with me. Take as much as you can and you will find you can take a bit more. It won't hurt you.' A growth in self-consciousness is not confined to religious poets, or even to

[*137*]

poets in general. It is a feature of all intellectual life since the Romantic period. It is peculiarly marked in religious poets and is particularly baneful with them since it is at war with the essential religious effort to deny the self. All the same, fine religious poetry has been written in this and the last century, certainly finer than any that the sixteenth century produced in England. This is an almost completely blank period for the lover of religious verse, in spite of the overwhelming concern with religion and the fervour of religious feeling that sent Protestants to the stake and Catholics to Tyburn. And it might well be argued that, applying the test of poetic quality strictly, the post-Christian ages, as they are sometimes oddly called, the nineteenth and twentieth centuries, have produced more religious poetry of high excellence than the so-called Ages of Faith. Professor George Kane has gone on record as saying that the 'Corpus Christi Carol' is the 'only surviving carol that can be called completely successful', and when we have added to it 'I sing of a maiden that is makeles', one or both of the poems that have for a refrain *Quia Amore Langueo*, some extracts from *Piers Plowman*, Chaucer's 'Ballade of Truth' (and perhaps the close of the *Troilus* and Theseus's speech from the *Knight's Tale*), Dunbar's 'On the Resurrection', and 'Woefully arrayed', there is not much else from the fourteenth and fifteenth centuries that one would wish to include in an anthology on the grounds of sheer poetic merit. Perhaps the Ages of Faith were unpropitious for the writing of religious poetry in being too propitious, and it was all too fatally easy then to write religious poetry that relied almost wholly on stock responses.

The truth would seem to be that conditions in different ages make more or less possible different ways of treating the subject. C. S. Lewis, in the review referred to, distinguished between the direct and the indirect method, dividing the direct into three kinds. First there was what he called the method of 'frontal assault': treat the subject as high as you can, exploit all the resources of language to express as nearly as possible what is inexpressible. Then there is the opposite, the method of 'humble sobriety': be as plain as you can, acknowledging that elaboration may diminish what simplicity at least will not disguise. Or there is the method of what Lewis called 'transferred classicism', what I would call 'spoiling the Egyptians', and what Johnson called 'trifling fictions': use the mythology of pagan poetry, and dignify and illustrate the subject by associating it with the traditions of great literature and the insights of the ancient world. All three kinds ask from the poet an unselfconscious approach to his subject and, except with very rare spirits, a reliance on a universal recognition of its importance and truth. But in every age there have also been poets that have employed a more indirect method, concentrating, as Lewis said, on the Incarnation, and leaving to be implied what it is that is incarnate, employing parable, or choosing as ostensible subject aspects of experience that are susceptible of a non-religious as well as a religious interpretation. In an age like the present, one would not expect to find great hymn-writers, or much use for the method of transferred classicism. Conditions are 'not propitious' for the frontal attack and the high style; and for transferred classicism we must substitute the use of mythologies more familiar to readers of the twentieth century than the mythology of Greece and Rome. Thus Eliot has turned to Shakespeare and Auden to Freud. If the direct method is attempted today it will take the form of what Lewis described as 'humble sobriety', as in Edwin Muir's simple and beautiful rendering of the annunciation: 'The angel and the girl are met'.[1] This is a poem of holy quiet and intense stillness, inspired perhaps by an Italian or Flemish painting of the girl in her solitary, modest room and the angel who has come to her from beyond time. As in many paintings of the subject, a moment of time is made to seem eternal.

> *The angel and the girl are met.*
> *Earth was the only meeting place.*
> *For the embodied never yet*
> *Travelled beyond the shore of space.*
> *The eternal spirits in freedom go.*

[1] 'The Annunciation', *Collected Poems* (1960), p. 223.

See, they have come together, see,
While the destroying minutes flow,
Each reflects the other's face
Till heaven in hers and earth in his
Shine steady there. He's come to her
From far beyond the farthest star,
Feathered through time. Immediacy
Of the strangest strangeness is the bliss
That from their limbs all movement takes.
Yet the increasing rapture brings
So great a wonder that it makes
Each feather tremble on his wings.

Outside the window footsteps fall
Into the ordinary day
And with the sun along the wall
Pursue their unreturning way.
Sound's perpetual roundabout
Rolls its numbered octaves out
And hoarsely grinds its battered tune.

But through the endless afternoon
These neither speak nor movement make,
But stare into their deepening trance
As if their gaze would never break.

Some readers of this poem may be at once reminded of an earlier, very different poem on the same accepted mystery of faith, the medieval lyric 'I sing of a maiden that is makeles':

He cam also stille
  Ther his moder was,
As dew in Aprille
  That falleth on the grass.

He cam also stille
  To his moderes bowr

> *As dew in Aprille*
> *That falleth on the flowr.*
>
> *He cam also stille*
> *Ther his moder lay,*
> *As dew in Aprille*
> *That falleth on the spray.*

The two poems have in common the sense of an event of mysterious and momentous importance taking place in absolute secrecy and complete quiet. To compare them in their treatment of the conception of the Son of God would involve considerations of metre and language and of poetic effects, the effect of irregular and regular rhyme, the effect of a studied flatness and the effect of lyric repetition with variation. It would also involve recognition of the differing traditions of love poetry the two poems are drawing on. The mother and maid of the medieval poem is the lady of courtly love poetry, admitting her lover in secret to her bower, while the girl of Edwin Muir's poem is a simple girl, and the poem has the tone and manner of a modern poem celebrating a moment 'in and out of time': such as a girl rapt in a mutual exchange of love with her lover while ordinary life goes on outside the window.

And what Lewis called the indirect method, by which the religious poet concentrates on the Incarnation and leaves the reader to infer what is incarnate is as open to the poet today as to his predecessor. The pathos and sweetness of the medieval lullaby carols, in which the destiny that awaits the weeping child its mother sings to and soothes gives poignancy to her love, has been beautifully caught in the lullaby that Auden wrote for his oratorio *For the Time Being*; but it has been transformed by including our modern insights into what we mean by 'the flesh', the perils of mother-love and anxiety, and the loneliness of the human condition:

> *O shut your bright eyes that mine must endanger*
> *With their watchfulness; protected by its shade*

Escape from my care: what can you discover
From my tender look but how to be afraid?
Love can but confirm the more it would deny.
    Close your bright eye.

Sleep. What have you learned from the womb that bore you
But an anxiety your Father cannot feel?
Sleep. What will the flesh that I gave do for you,
Or my mother love, but tempt you from His will?
Why was I chosen to teach His Son to weep?
    Little One sleep.

Dream. In human dreams earth ascends to Heaven
Where no one need pray nor ever feel alone.
In your first few hours of life here, O have you
Chosen already what death must be your own?
How soon will you start on the Sorrowful Way?
    Dream while you may.

The poet has accepted modern selfconsciousness and created a poem in which Mary and her Son become the archetypal Mother and Son and the mother's role is contrasted with the father's. Through this a fresh insight is suggested into the accepted mystery of God made Man. The poem could not have been written before the mid-twentieth century. It is post-Freud in conception, post-Eliot in rhythm and vocabulary. As the medieval writer of a religious lullaby carol picked up from the melancholy secular lullaby in the Kildare manuscript his refrain 'Lullay, lullay, litel child, Qui wepest thou so sore', and transferred its sense of the sorrowfulness of human life to the destiny of the Man of Sorrows, so Auden begins from any mother and any son. I do not doubt that in the twenty-first century, equally, poets who accept the limitations of religious poetry will find ways of using the idiom of their own day to render their vision of religious truth and their sense of religious commitment.

II

Secular and Divine Poetry

Religious thought and practice, forms of worship and methods of prayer, personal religious experience and religious feelings, and religious conceptions of the good life are no more static through the centuries than are the arts. Both change and develop by reason of their own inner principles of growth, and in accordance with, and in interaction with, social changes and intellectual movements. The relations of religion and of the arts to society are complex and variable, an interaction in which it is rarely possible to discern a simple sequence of cause and effect. The relations of religion to art and secular learning are equally complex and variable, art and learning drawing fresh inspiration and discovering new directions from religion, religion taking up and using the secular achievements of civilization. But with poetry, at any rate in Christian Europe, whatever the relation of religion and poetry in primitive times and in other cultures, the traffic has been mostly one way. Eliot was fundamentally right in speaking of religious poetry as a 'department of poetry', for the religious poet in England has mostly taken up and adapted to his special subject the dominant themes and dominant forms of secular poetry rather than invented new themes and forms for secular poets to copy. Much English religious poetry is a form of parody, if we use the word in its original technical sense of a fitting of new words to existing tunes, or the adaptation of the form and style of one work to become the vehicle of another with a different subject-matter, and forget the usual modern sense which implies that such imitation or adaptation is for the purposes of mockery and satire.

[*143*]

The reason for this is obvious. Christianity, the historic religion of Europe, was born into a world of great intellectual and artistic achievement, with which it had to come to terms. From the earliest times the Christian attitude to secular learning and secular art was Janus-like, or double-faced, corresponding to the contrary strains in Christian thought: the impulse to deny the world and all secular values, even the highest, and the impulse to embrace the world and sanctify its values. The two strains, denial of the world and affirmation of the world, existing together in tension, are perhaps essential to every religion; but in Christianity the tension is explicit, and the conflict of attitudes between individuals and within individuals is there from the beginning; St. Paul, on the one hand declaring that he wishes to know nothing 'save Jesus Christ and him crucified', and on the other quoting to the Athenians from their own poets. The cry 'What has Christ to do with Apollo?', or 'with Ingeld?',[1] is a recurring cry through the centuries. Equally strong is the impulse to see in Apollo, or Hercules, or other gods and heroes of pagan legend, types of Christ and his saints, and to bring to the feet of Christ the treasures of human learning and the glories of art. The Christian may either flee the Egypt of worldly vanities, or 'spoil the Egyptians' to enrich the service of the God of Israel.

The most striking example of a 'spoiling of the Egyptians' is the medieval carol, which most people think of at once as the most characteristic form of medieval religious verse. So successful in this case were the religious writers in appropriating to pious uses the carol form, that the word has in popular usage quite lost its original sense and come to mean anything, hymn, song, ballad or carol proper, that can be sung at Christmas. The carol was originally a dance-song, sung by dancers, in a ring or in a row holding hands, who sang the burden while their leader sang the

[1] Alcuin, writing to a bishop of Lindisfarne in the eighth century, 'reproves the monks for their fondness for old stories about heathen kings, who are now lamenting their sins in Hell: "in the Refectory," he says, "the Bible should be read: the lector heard, not the harper: patristic sermons rather than pagan songs. For what has Ingeld to do with Christ?" (R. W. Chambers, *Beowulf*, 2nd edn., 1932, p. 22.)

stanzas. Stanza and burden is what marks the carol form and
carols had no necessary connection with Christmas, except that
Christmas was a natural season for merry-making and feasting,
food being plentiful as it was not at Easter after the winter. Carols
and carolling were the subject of many denunciations and prohibitions by the Church, partly because carolling had pre-
Christian roots and was a remnant of pagan customs. It was
possibly connected with witchcraft, for witches danced in circles
'hand in hand'. Partly also, it was denounced from fear of 'lewd-
ness' following on the singing of 'lewd songs', and of violence
following on excited merry-making. That carolling had originally
no 'odour of sanctity', but rather the reverse, is shown by the
famous story of the dancers of Colbek, who carolled in the church-
yard on Christmas Eve. The priest came out and ordered them to
stop and come in to hear the service. When they refused he cursed
them, so that they were unable to break their circle or stop danc-
ing for a whole year. They danced in their forbidden circle
through all Germany to the wonder and amusement of all who
saw them, as a dreadful object lesson of the punishment due to the
sin of carolling. It was this despised and feared form that was
taken up and baptized, almost certainly by the Friars. The same
phenomenon can be observed in Italy, where Jacopone da Todi
composed his vernacular *Laude* in forms and to music familiar to
the people; and in France, where the earliest known composer of
Noels was a Franciscan. In England, wherever we come across a
name in connection with carols, the name is usually that of a
Franciscan. The carol represents the simplest form of parody:
the writing of new words to an old tune. And it is perhaps foolish
to complain that the vast mass of carols are not highly successful
poetically, and that our affection for them is largely due to their
sentimental associations and to the charm of the melodies to
which they are sung. I am not sure, in spite of Professor Kane,
that it is even true. What shines out from the medieval carol, and
from other medieval religious lyrics, is the intense poetry of the
subject-matter, the extreme expressiveness of the story of Christ's
life and death as a revelation of the nature of God.

Christianity stands out among the great religions of the world by reason of its narrative and historical content. The Christian revelation does not take the form of 'This the Lord said', but of 'This the Lord did, this he was, this he suffered'. The stress of medieval religious poetry is on this, and not on the religious feelings and experience of individual men. The feelings expressed are common, unindividualized: praise, thanksgiving, sorrow, love responding to love. They are what the writer assumes that all men should feel confronted with these facts: the King of Heaven in an oxen-stall, the Lord of Glory suffering a shameful and agonizing death. The stress is always more on the facts than on the feelings: on the marvel of God's coming to man rather than on man's attempt to come to God. Although it is true that many carols render their subject in a kind of sing-song, with plentiful inversions and otiose words to fill out the line and keep the tune, at their best the medieval lyrics render it with a transparency that silences criticism. Adapting the words of a favourite medieval simile—'For as the sun shines through glass, So Jesus in his Mother was'—we might say that the essential poetry of the Christian revelation shines through a transparent veil of verse. It is characteristic of medieval poetry for Christ to speak to man from the Cross, or for his mother, at the Cross's foot, to plead for man's pity and love, not for man to meditate on Christ's death for his sins. What God has done and does, not what man feels, is the characteristic medieval theme. A poem such as Donne's 'Good Friday: Riding Westward' is inconceivable in the fourteenth century. It is 'Man's soul' that Christ languishes for, and 'Man' that he pleads with; the address is to the soul of each and every man, not to an individual soul that he pursues through its subtle, personal ways. The appeal is magnificently general. In this generality the finest religious poetry of the fourteenth and fifteenth centuries is classic, and invites comparison with the finest religious poetry of the eighteenth century, the great century of the English Hymn. Much has been written lately of the medieval roots of the religious poetry of the metaphysical poets of the seventeenth century; but the Wesleys have more in common with the writers of our carols and of most of our medieval religious lyrics than Donne and Herbert have. They were actuated by much the same motives as actuated the Franciscans: to replace secular by pious songs, using the secular idiom and secular melodies, and to set forth the central mysteries of the faith in a manner that makes clear their universal relevance. If the medieval poet rejoices in salvation, it is in the common salvation wrought by the Redeemer of the human race; if he presents Christ as pleading from the Cross, he presents him as pleading to all who pass by; if he presents penitence, it is the penitence of all Adam's sons that he presents. Thus, in a touching lullaby to the infant Saviour, although at first it is a single speaker that asks for mercy, he fades into Adam and then into all mankind:[1]

> *Lullay, lullay, litel child,*
> *Qui wepest thou so sore?*
>
> *Lullay, lullay, litel child,*
> *Thou that were so sterne and wild*
> *Nou art become meke and mild*
>   *To saven that was forlore.*
>
> *But for my senne I wot it is*
> *That Godis Sone suffret this;*
> *Merci, Lord! I have do mis;*
>   *Iwis, I wile no more.*
>
> *Ayenis my Fadris wille I ches*
> *An appel with a reuful res;*
> *Werfore myn heritage I les,*
>   *And nou thou wepist therfore.*
>
> *An appel I tok of a tre;*
> *God it hadde forboden me;*

[1] Printed by R. L. Greene, in *A Selection of English Carols* (1962), from MS. Advocates 18.7.21 in the National Library of Scotland, dated 1372.

Werfore I sulde dampned be,
  Yif thi weping ne wore.

Lullay, for wo, thou litel thing,
Thou litel barun, thou litel king;
Mankindde is cause of thi murning
  That thou has loved so yore.

For man, that thou has ay loved so,
Yet saltu suffren peines mo,
In heved, in feet, in hondis to,
  And yet wepen wel more.

That peine us make of senne fre;
That peine us bringge, Jesu, to the;
That peine us helpe ay to fle
  The wikkede fendes lore.

A more interesting way of sanctifying the secular than this method of parody, the writing of new words to old tunes, is the treatment of religious themes in the style and mood in which secular poetry treats the highest secular ideals. It is more interesting because it is frequently not conscious and deliberate, but the result of a natural impulse to render the sense of the divine in terms of the highest and most valued human experiences. One of the most striking features of English medieval poetry is the persistence in England of the old heroic tradition, alongside with, and intermingled with, the chivalric and the courtly mode of feeling. This gives Malory's treatment of the Arthur stories, as late as the fifteenth century, an epic as well as a romantic beauty. The same survival of earlier and sterner conceptions can be seen in religious verse.

The characteristic medieval stress on the mysteries of the faith, on the things done for man, is wonderfully rendered in what is perhaps the finest extant Anglo-Saxon religious poem, *The Dream of the Rood*, and, centuries later, in the most powerfully imagined and expressed section of *Piers Plowman*, the *passus* that tells of the Harrowing of Hell. In both Christ appears as the Hero. *The Dream of the Rood* is a parallel in the vernacular to the magnificent hymns that Venantius Fortunatus wrote to celebrate the coming of the relics of the true Cross to Poitiers: *Vexilla regis prodeunt, Fulget crucis mysterium*, and *Pange, lingua, gloriosi proelium certaminis*. As in the hymns, the tree is still a tree that once grew in the forest among other trees. It was honoured above all other trees, but in being honoured it was outraged. The Anglo-Saxon poet makes far more strongly than the Latin poet, and indeed more strongly than any poet I know of, the contrast between the brilliant jewelled rood that men honour and the tree of shame, the gallows of the Lord, between the splendours of Christian ritual and the ignominious facts of the Gospel story. The paradox of victory won in apparent defeat is the theme; the strength of the crucified Saviour rather than his sufferings is the poet's concern. The Latin poem sees Christ as King: *Regnavit ligno Deus*. The Anglo-Saxon poet sees him as Hero, stripping himself for the fight, and mounting the Cross of his own free will to redeem mankind and perform God's strange work of remaking man. An equal firmness, a comparable heroism, is shown in the created thing chosen to be the instrument of salvation. For all its horror at the role it is called to play, and for all its compassion, it stands firm and braces itself to bear its Lord up for the battle. The Latin poet saw Christ as King, the calm, robed figure of early crucifixes, with arms spread out in power and blessing, and crowned head looking out in majesty upon the world, not the fainting, drooping figure, hanging from the nails, of the later Middle Ages. The Anglo-Saxon poet sees him as a warrior, enduring all. Endurance is the great heroic virtue of Anglo-Saxon poetry from *Beowulf* to *The Battle of Maldon*.

Some six hundred years later Langland showed Christ as a knight, jousting for man's soul, and as King and Warrior coming to redeem his own. The sternness of earlier Christian thought which saw Christ less as the representative of suffering humanity, bearing the punishment for men's sins, and more as the King of Glory paying the ransom to redeem mankind from the devil's power, survives in Langland in a century dominated by Franciscan gentleness, in which the prevailing images are of the babe on his mother's knee and the Man of Sorrows. In the wonderful scene in No Man's Land, the region between heaven and hell, on Holy Saturday, Christ appears as a great light shining in darkness coming to redeem his blood brothers, having paid the ransom for them as a King should. Many students of medieval literature have commented on the remarkable persistence and popularity of the theme of the Harrowing of Hell in English poetry and the survival in England of the older doctrine of the Atonement, familiar from such ancient office hymns as 'Ye choirs of New Jerusalem', as the rescue of humanity from the power of the devil. The figure of Christ as humanity's champion, rather than as sacrificial victim, not making satisfaction to God for man's sins, but outwitting and defeating his and mankind's enemies, survives into the later Middle Ages because of the continuing strength of the old heroic tradition. It is found as late as the turn of the fifteenth century in Dunbar's poem on the Resurrection, a rare theme in Christian art and poetry. The poem is in stanza form, with a Latin refrain, and employs classical allusions in the Renaissance manner in its third stanza; but it echoes constantly the old alliterative line and embodies the old heroic vision of Christ the Champion, treading down his and our foes.

> *Done is a battell on the dragon blak,*
> *Our campioun Chryst confountet hes his force;*
> *The yettis of hell ar brokin with a crak,*
> *The signe triumphall rasit is of the croce,*
> *The divillis trymmillis with hiddous voce,*
> *The saulis ar borrowit and to the blis can go,*
> *Christ with his blud our ransonis dois indoce:*   (endorse)
> Surrexit dominus de sepulchro.
>
> *Dungin is the deidly dragon Lucifer,*
> *The crewall serpent with the mortall stang,*
> *The auld kene tegir with his teith on char*   (ajar)

Quhilk in a wait hes lyne for us so lang,
Thinking to grip us in his clowis strang:
The mercifule lord wald nocht that it wer so,
He maid him for to felye of that fang: (fail of that booty)
Surrexit dominus de sepulchro.

He for our saik that sufferit to be slane
And lyk a lamb in sacrifice wes dicht,
Is lyk a lyone rissin up agane,
And as a gyane raxit him on hicht:
Sprungin is Aurora radius and bricht,
On loft is gone the glorius Appollo,
The blisfull day depairtit fro the nycht:
Surrexit dominus de sepulchro.

The grit victour againe is rissin on hicht
That for our querrell to the deth wes woundit;
The sone that wox all paill now schynis bricht,
And, dirknes clerit, our fayth is now refoundit:
The knell of mercy fra the hevin is soundit,
The Cristin ar deliverit of thair wo,
The Jewis and thair errour ar confoundit:
Surrexit dominus de sepulchro.

The fo is chasit, the battell is done ceis,
The presone brokin, the jevellouris fleit and flemit,
The weir is gon, confermit is the peis,
The fetteris lowsit, and the dungeoun temit,
The ransoun maid, the presoneris redemit,
The feild is win, ourcummin is the fo,
Dispulit of the tresur that he yemit:
Surrexit dominus de sepulchro.

This is a splendid example of what C. S. Lewis called the 'frontal assault' or 'going as high as you can'.

A more familiar image is the image of Christ the Lover, the

wooer of man's soul. All the forms of medieval love poetry—the *chanson d'aventure*, the *lauda*, the *plaint*—are turned, as all over Europe, to the service of religion. The concepts of courtesy, of chivalry and of chivalric love, are employed to illuminate the Christian message of divine love, and to give to the figures of the Christian story the grace of contemporary ideals. The praises of the Virgin echo the praises of the 'Lady' of courtly love. The exquisite lyric 'I sing of a maiden' echoes, in its stress on stillness and secrecy, the necessity for secrecy in love. This is one of the few medieval poems that has had to endure explication *à la mode*, because of the beautiful ambiguity of its phrasing: the doubt of who it was that came 'al so stille', and the double meaning of 'makeles'. The language is the language of love poetry and the suggestion is of the lady, of her own choice, admitting her lover to her bower. The subtlety and sweetness of this poem contrasts with the splendid directness with which Christ, the Knight-Lover, speaks in another anonymous poem of the fourteenth century:

Love me brought,
And love me wrought,
Man, to be thy fere.
Love me fed,
And love me led,
And love me letted here.

Love me slew,
And love me drew,
And love me laid on bere.
Love is my peace,
For love I ches,
Man to buyen dere.

No dread thee nought,
I have thee sought,
Bothen day and night.
To haven thee,

Well is me,
I have thee wonnen in fight.[1]

The most beautiful of the love poems of Christ to the soul is one
of the two fourteenth-century poems that share the refrain *Quia
Amore Langueo*. The tradition that interpreted the Song of Songs
allegorically blends here with the concept of Christ the Knight-
Lover, suffering as love's servant for a mistress that disdains him
and is unmoved by his sufferings. The form is that of a *chanson
d'aventure* in which the poet overhears a love-tale or love-complaint.
In the other poem with this refrain the speaker of the plaint is the
Virgin. The two poems are quite distinct, except for their common refrain, and it is impossible to say which is the earlier and
served as model, or, indeed, whether one is modelled on the other
at all. Both are exceedingly moving in their presentation of the
medieval ideal of love as humble service; but, in my judgment,
the one in which Christ is the speaker is the more touching and
sublime as an expression of the humility of love that seeks and
suffers, and, although rebuffed, still offers itself.

The interaction of the secular and the divine in English
medieval poetry attains a mysterious beauty in the Corpus Christi
carol, extant in more than one form. In its finest version, which
would seem also to be the earliest, it has a haunting refrain that
suggests folk-lore, and in all its versions, it has a rhetorical
pattern, the climbing figure, that is familiar from nursery rhymes,
the pattern of 'The House that Jack built'. Although it conforms
to the definition of a carol, being in stanzas with a burden, it is not
in the usual carol form: the stanzas are not of four lines, but are
couplets. This gives it a tautness and a laconic severity that is very
different from the tone and pace of most carols. I find it difficult to
accept the suggestion of Professor R. L. Greene, to whom all
students of carols are so deeply indebted, that this carol is concerned with the displacement of Katherine of Aragon by Anne

[1] Printed from MS. Advocates 18.7.21 in the National Library of
Scotland by Carleton Brown, *Religious Lyrics of the Fourteenth Century*
(1924, p. 84). I have not preserved the spelling here or in the following
carol, thinking it might mislead readers.

Boleyn in the affections of Henry VIII, Anne's badge being a white falcon. On this interpretation the maid who kneels by the bed on which Christ the Knight lies bleeding is Henry's rejected wife, who occupied herself in her exile from court with lamentations and devotions; and the poem was written by partisans of Katherine to arouse sympathy for her in her cruel situation. Others have seen a connection between the carol and the Grail legend. Whatever its origins, it appeals to us today because of its tone of mystery. Unlike most medieval poems it is indirect, hints rather than makes clear. It allows us—behind the images of chivalry, the hall with its sombre hangings, the richly decked bed, the bleeding knight, the weeping maiden, and the magical stone with its sacred inscription—to discover for ourselves what significance best fits the meaning we attach to the words *Corpus Christi*:

> *Lully, lulley; lully, lulley;*
> *The falcon hath borne my make away.*
>
> *He bare him up, he bare him down;*
> *He bare him into an orchard brown*
>
> *In that orchard there was an hall,*
> *That was hanged with purple and pall.*
>
> *And in that hall there was a bed;*
> *It was hanged with gold so red.*
>
> *And in that bed there lyeth a knight,*
> *His woundes bleeding day and night.*
>
> *By that beddes side there kneleth a may,*
> *And she wepeth both night and day.*
>
> *And by that beddes side there standeth a stone,*
> Corpus Christi *written thereon.*

At first there seems some contradiction to the view that the religious verse of a period will parody, or adapt, or reflect the dominant modes and forms of its secular verse in the fact that the eighteenth century, which is not on the whole a period distinguished for its lyric verse, has been rightly called 'The Century of Divine Songs'. But the hymn, which is the great eighteenth-century lyric form, is a lyric of a special kind. With its great roll-call of hymn-writers, Addison, Watts, Charles Wesley, Cowper, the eighteenth century rivals the medieval period in giving expression to what I have called 'the essential poetry of the Christian revelation'. In the poetry of personal and individual devotion it provides little that is worth reading. If we were to judge by this century alone, we should agree with Johnson that 'intercourse between God and the human soul cannot be poetical'. But Johnson carefully distinguished 'poetical devotion', in which his age is weak, from didactic poetry, 'in which the doctrines of religion are defended', and from praising the Creator by praising his works. The so-called 'Age of Reason', if we reckon it from the Restoration, can provide examples of the fact that Johnson noted that 'he who has the happy power of arguing in verse will not lose it because his subject is sacred'. Our greatest argumentative poet, John Dryden, in the opening lines of *Religio Laici* and in his defence of the authority of revelation in *The Hind and the Panther*, argues with fervour for reason's limits. In addition, as we would expect from a century famous for moral and didactic verse, we find noble expression of the religious temper of mind, as distinct from religious experience, a tone of sober and settled conviction. No finer expression of the religious attitude to life can be found in any century than the moving close of Johnson's own *Vanity of Human Wishes*; and no more touching tribute to the primacy of other worldly values in our judgment of human achievement than his lines to the memory of his obscure friend Dr. Robert Levet. And, though some of the attempts to praise the Creator by praising his works lack exaltation and seem rather to add a pious varnish to an essentially secular theme, the eighteenth century, in which the poetry of natural description became a poetic kind in its own right, instead of being merely a background to narrative or meditative verse, achieved one glorious celebration of the Creator of the natural world in Smart's *Song to David*. In one other thing also, beside the hymn, the eighteenth century has affinities with the medieval period. It can provide what the early seventeenth century, for all its variety and richness in religious verse, hardly attempts and, if it does, does feebly, religious satire. Pope's Sir Balaam is a masterly portrait of what Donne calls 'a practical atheist', and Holy Willie in his prayer rivals Chaucer's Pardoner as a study of the corruption of religion.

But the glory of the eighteenth century in religious poetry lies in its hymns. A hymn is a distinct kind of poetry, and while one must own that many of the hymns in hymn-books are very doubtfully poetry, it must also be said that many of the hymns in modern hymnals are not really hymns. A complaint is often made that hymns use exaggerated language, that they cannot be sung with sincerity, and that it is absurd for a congregation of ordinary wayfaring Christians to be expected to sing sentiments that even saints can hardly be expected to feel habitually. There is a well-known joke about the Duchess singing in a warm tremolo 'Were the whole realm of nature mine, That were an offering far too small' while she hunted in her purse for sixpence to put in the plate. But the joke is misconceived. A hymn is not intended to express the personal situation or personal warmth of feeling of an individual singer, but a common ideal of Christian feeling and sentiment which the congregation acknowledges as an ideal. A poem such as Donne's 'Hymn to God the Father' is most unsuitably included in a hymnal and Newman's 'Lead kindly Light' is not at all suited to congregational singing. A hymn should present religious doctrine, religious duty or religious mythology; and it should present it in a form suited to congregational use: that is, in a single repeating stanza that can be set to an easily memorable tune. It has a certain function to perform. As George Sampson said in a famous British Academy lecture,[1] the purpose

[1] 'The Century of Divine Songs', *Proceedings of the British Academy*, Vol. XXIX (1944).

of a hymn is to create the sense of belonging to a continuing fellowship. It should not be too individual, too original, in its images and phrasing. Its symbols should be stock symbols, from the Bible and the liturgy. They are used to give men a sense of the traditions they inherit, of which they are also custodians for future generations. People are rightly and instinctively conservative about hymns and the tunes that they are sung to. They do not want fresh insights from hymns, but a sense of their unity with their fellow-believers, with their fathers and forefathers, and with those who will come after them. The characteristic virtues of much eighteenth-century poetry and many characteristic tenets of eighteenth-century criticism go far to explain why the eighteenth century is the great age of the English hymn. Johnson's exaltation of the judgment of the common reader, the praise of 'the grandeur of generality' that underlies so much of his criticism, and his belief that men need more to be reminded of known truths than told of new belong to the same age as the Wesleys' determination to provide poetry that the ordinary Christian could sing to tunes that he knew. The strength of style, the impersonal majesty and muscular plainness of the best eighteenth-century hymns are qualities they share with the best secular verse of the period.

The great period of English hymnody begins soon after the Restoration, with Bishop Ken's hymns for morning and evening, Nahum Tate's 'While shepherds watched their flocks by night', and Dryden's vigorous and beautiful rendering of the *Veni Creator Spiritus*. These are forerunners. The movement may be said to have become established when Addison took up the question of divine poetry in the *Spectator*. He began in No. 441 by supplying, at the close of an essay on reliance on God, a translation or extended paraphrase of the twenty-third psalm. Two months later, at the end of an essay on gratitude, he attempted an original hymn: 'When all thy Mercies, O my God, My rising Soul surveys'. In a later essay, on the impressions of divine power and wisdom in the universe, he ended by quoting the Psalmist, 'The heavens declare the glory of God', and thinking that 'such a bold and sublime manner of Thinking furnishes very noble Matter for an Ode', provided one: 'The Spacious Firmament on high'. In No. 489 he allowed 'a correspondent' to quote 'a Divine Ode, made by a Gentleman upon the Conclusion of his Travels': his own 'How are thy Servants blest, O Lord'; and in No. 513 he adopted the same subterfuge and printed from another 'correspondent', an 'Excellent Man in Holy Orders', a letter that ended with a hymn composed in sickness: 'When rising from the Bed of Death'. But in No. 461 Steele printed a letter from a genuine correspondent who, declaring himself inspired by Addison's example, offered a 'Translation without Paraphrase' in imitation of the 114th Psalm. The author was Dr. Isaac Watts, a Dissenting minister, whose *Hymns and Spiritual Songs*, which had appeared in 1707, may be said to have established the hymn as an essential element in English worship. Reading Watts in bulk is not inspiring and one has to agree with Johnson that 'the paucity of topics enforces perpetual repetition' and the monotony of the simple stanza form soon wearies the reader. Even so, again and again one is struck by the felicity of his phrasing:

> *My best-Beloved keeps his Throne*
> *On Hills of Light, in Worlds unknown;*
> *But he descends, and shows his Face*
> *In the young Gardens of his Grace.*

To read Watts through in bulk is to wrong him. His glory is to have written two hymns that have passed into the permanent language of Christian worship: the majestic 'O God our Help in Ages past', a psalm paraphrase that can face Coverdale's prose, and the poignant 'When I survey the wondrous Cross'. Almost as beautiful, for its purity of style, is 'There is a Land of pure Delight', and the lullaby from the *Divine Songs for Children* that inspired Blake. Watts retains, along with his chaste eighteenth-century diction, something of the 'holy amorousness' of seventeenth-century poetry, as in 'Sweet Muse, descend and bless the shade'.

Two things characterize the Methodist hymn, which continued the tradition established by Watts: emphasis on the message of salvation, on the good news of the Redemption wrought once for all by the Son of God, Very God of Very God, and dependence on the language of Scripture. They may be praised in words that Donne used, although in a secular context: 'They rest on what the Catholic voice doth teach.' From the enormous mass of Charles Wesley's hymns, one may point to the hymns for the great feasts —Christmas, Easter, Ascension—or to such noble expressions of thanksgiving as 'O for a thousand tongues to sing My dear Redeemer's praise', or to such a splendid call to the ardours of the Christian life as 'Soldiers of Christ arise', or to the beautiful Eucharistic hymns, 'Author of life Divine' and 'Victim Divine, thy Grace we crave', or to such an exquisite example of 'parody' as 'Love Divine, all loves excelling', to be sung to the tune that Purcell wrote to Dryden's 'Fairest Isle, all isles excelling'. As in some of the great Latin Office Hymns, the strength and the poetry of the Christian myth of salvation freely offered to all, and of the great hope for the world, shines through a language that in no way veils or plays with its intrinsic power. The eighteenth-century hymn reflects the poetic ideals of the age in its reliance on what is held to be known truth, its economy and directness of language, and its decorum. They are hymns that can be sung without embarrassment by all Christians. If I over-rate their value as poems, and if, as some would claim with Johnson, their excellence as hymns detracts from their value as poems, nobody, I imagine, would deny the moving beauty of one poem by Charles Wesley, inappropriately sung as a hymn in a shortened version: the mystical poem called 'Wrestling Jacob'.

> *Come, O Thou Traveller unknown,*
> *Whom still I hold, but cannot see,*
> *My Company before is gone,*
> *And I am left alone with Thee,*
> *With Thee all Night I mean to stay,*
> *And wrestle till the Break of Day.*

Of this poem, John Wesley said, in his obituary tribute to his brother, that Dr. Watts did not scruple to say that it was worth

'all the verses he himself had written'. It has the masculine plainness of the best eighteenth-century poetry, makes vivid use of
Scriptural language and employs, with thrilling effect, strong
repetition. It is, perhaps, too long, as many mystical poems are;
yet it keeps a note of urgency and achieves a reversal of great
poignancy at its close, in that triumph mingles with the acceptance of the mysterious laming of Jacob, who wrestled all night
with the angel and ever after 'halted on one thigh'.

The best Wesley hymns are classic. An altogether wilder note is
struck by Christopher Smart. Where the Wesleys, even in their
poorer hymns, seem to go unerringly for the bull's-eye, Smart is
one of the great hit-or-miss poets. When he hits the result is at
once graceful and astonishing, when he fails he achieves complete
bathos. In addition to his rhapsodic *Song to David*, and the dithy-
rambic 'Rejoice in the Lamb', he produced a metrical version of
the psalms that does not rise above the dreary average of metrical
psalms, and a volume of *Hymns and Spiritual Songs for the Fasts and
Festivals of the Church of England*. Some of these, such as that on the
uninspiring subject of the deliverance from the Gunpowder Plot,
are rambling nonsense, even though almost all have fine moments;
but there is one poem in this volume of which I would not have a
word different: the Hymn on the Nativity, with its astonishing
alternations between a charming pastoralism and sublime affirmation. It ranks with Charles Wesley's 'Hark how all the Welkin
rings' and John Byrom's 'Christians awake! Salute the Happy
Morn' as an eighteenth-century celebration of 'the mystery of
love':

> *Where is this stupendous stranger,*
> *Swains of Solyma, advise,*
> *Lead me to my Master's manger,*
> *Shew me where my Saviour lies?*

> *O Most Mighty! O MOST HOLY!*
> *Far beyond the seraph's thought,*
> *Art thou then so mean and lowly*
> *As unheeded prophets taught?*

Secular and Divine Poetry

O the magnitude of meekness!
   Worth from worth immortal sprung;
O the strength of infant weakness,
   If eternal is so young!

If so young and thus eternal,
   Michael tune the shepherd's reed,
Where the scenes are ever vernal,
   And the loves be love indeed!

See the God blasphem'd and doubted
   In the schools of Greece and Rome;
See the pow'rs of darkness routed,
   Taken at their utmost gloom.

Nature's decorations glisten
   Far above their usual trim;
Birds on box and laurels listen,
   As so near the cherubs hymn.

Boreas now no longer winters
   On the desolated coast;
Oaks no more are riv'n in splinters
   By the whirlwind and his host.

Spinks and ouzels sing sublimely,
   'We too have a Saviour born',
Whiter blossoms burst untimely
   On the blest Mosaic thorn.

God all-bounteous, all-creative,
   Whom no ills from good dissuade,
Is incarnate, and a native
   Of the very world he made.

With the immense changes in human feeling and in the whole

conception of the nature of poetry and of the poet's task that occur all over Europe in the revolutionary period at the end of the eighteenth century, one thing that is lost is the capacity to write public poetry of any kind: poetry that expresses national senti-ment, or agreed ethical conceptions, as much as poetry that ex-presses common religious feelings and accepted religious beliefs. The poet becomes an explorer and discoverer rather than a maker. Personal vision and personal truth of feeling is demanded of him. During the nineteenth century the feeling grows that the lyric is the highest form of poetry, the only true poetical kind; and the term 'lyric' is redefined, losing its original connection with music and becoming identified with the expression of personal feelings. One would not expect, therefore, to find in the religious poetry of the nineteenth century success in the hymn, the celebration, or what C. S. Lewis called the 'frontal attack'. Religious poetry be-comes the poetry of personal faith, personal discovery and per-sonal doubt. Religious experience finds sublime expression in many passages of Wordsworth's *Prelude*, and religious faith and dedication burns in Shelley's poetry. There is no comparable ex-pression of the sublime or the ardent in those whose religious life is nourished by the Christian tradition. Nor, I think, after Words-worth and Shelley, are such qualities often found in religious poetry outside the Christian tradition, or in nineteenth-century poetry generally. Although a great deal of the poetry of the nine-teenth century is infused with religious feeling, it is difficult to find many religious poems of the highest excellence, and the poetry of religious devotion is individual in a sense different from what one intends when one speaks of the poets of the seventeenth century and praises the individuality of their religious verse. In the seven-teenth century, poets display a strongly individual handling of what are common themes, so that there is a blending of 'tradition and the individual talent'. In the nineteenth century the poet is expected to create not only his poem but also his subject-matter. The conceptions as well as the treatment have to bear the motto 'All my own work'. If the seventeenth-century poet is like an architect, using materials provided by others and designing his building on an accepted model, the nineteenth-century poet is brick-maker, quarryer, bricklayer and stonemason as well as architect. His building is often endangered by some weakness in the brick or softness in the stone, as well as by the required independence of architectural tradition.

A great deal of the religious poetry of the nineteenth century is, it must be owned, sentimental. The same charge can be brought against much of the secular poetry of the age. There is an oppressive domesticity in many Victorian novels and in much Victorian poetry. This is reflected in the stress in much of the poetry of religious sentiment on family pieties, as if the essence of religion could be summed in the image of the family walking to church of a Sunday, and the promise of eternal life meant merely the promise of an endless family reunion. The Victorians interpreted perhaps too literally the command that we should become as little children, and their conception of the child was in many cases a very limited one. Much of the poetry of religious feeling is nostalgic. Nostalgia is the tone of much of that poetry of doubt in which religious need is expressed, often very movingly. In argumentative and apologetic verse the nineteenth-century poets lack the resonance and conviction of the ratiocinative verse of the seventeenth and eighteenth centuries. They are either too wistful, with Tennyson, or too naggingly insistent, as is Browning. Uncertainty of tone reflects the intellectual uncertainty of the age.

Browning is much less interesting and successful in his attempts at apologetic in *Christmas Eve* and *Easter Day* than in his attempts to express religious feelings and experiences in some of his dramatic monologues. He is liberated by the indirect approach. In 'Saul', 'Cleon', 'Karshish' and 'A Death in the Desert', and in dramatic lyrics such as 'Abt Vogler' or 'Rabbi Ben Ezra', he found a form that enabled him to handle religious experience with imaginative conviction and sympathy and with the objectivity that earlier ages had found in the use of myth. History gave to Browning what mythology had given to earlier poets who needed to approach their subject obliquely. History and the form of the dramatic monologue also gave to Browning the oppor-

[*163*]

tunity to employ his genius as a satirist on religious subjects. His 'Soliloquy in a Spanish Cloister' and his 'Johannes Agricola in Meditation' are satires on types that appear in every century, presented as historical personages; while in 'Bishop Blougram's Apology' and 'Mr. Sludge the Medium' he explored, through dramatic impersonations, the psychology of the religious world-ling and of the religious charlatan.

In spite of all that made the nineteenth century in many ways an unpropitious age for the writing of religious poetry in my sense of the term, it produced in Hopkins a poet of stature who is fully of his age and yet transcends its limitations, accepting the challenge of making poetry directly out of the intercourse of God and the human soul; and in Christina Rossetti and Emily Brontë it produced two poets who, in opposite ways, escaped from the prevailing tameness. Hopkins is deeply a Victorian in his profound feeling for nature, his naturalist's eye and ear, and in his sensuousness. He is also Victorian in his uninhibited warmth of feeling, in such poems as 'In the Valley of the Elwy', 'Felix Randall' and 'The Bugler's First Communion'. But he brings to Victorian poetry an intellectual severity that it otherwise rather lacks, and a sense of the heroic. In his concentration on the ardours and endurances of the spiritual life, as opposed to its consolations, in his feeling for the tragic rather than the pathetic, his knowledge of the loneliness and pain that is involved in man's effort to be born again, and of the terror that lurks behind such often easily used words as 'Almighty God', Hopkins sounds notes that we hardly hear elsewhere in his century in English poetry. In his efforts to forge for himself a new vocabulary and new rhythms he wrestles in his own way with the legacy of romanticism that demanded that the form of a poem should be as original as its subject, its thought and its sensibility: that every poem should have a form that was 'the true voice of feeling'. The idiosyncrasy of Hopkins's style, his extreme unlikeness to his contemporaries that made him, when he was discovered, a kind of 'honorary twentieth-century poet', is in itself Victorian. After the eighteenth century the conception of a common poetic style breaks down and each poet has to achieve his own 'decorum'. What seems in Hopkins's poetic style a greater eccentricity, a wilfulness much exceeding, for instance, Browning's, is the corollary of his comparative spiritual isolation in his age. We are always conscious of strain and effort; and, as he himself confessed, we 'miss'

> *The roll, the rise, the carol, the creation.*

Nobody would claim that Christina Rossetti is a poet of the stature of Hopkins. She is precisely what we mean by a minor poet of the first water. She was deeply pious and found a satisfaction, untroubled by doubts, in High Anglicanism. She comes very close to some poets of the seventeenth century in her complete acceptance of the Christian tradition, and in the exquisiteness of her art. She had a fine ear and a natural feeling for language. Her style is idiomatic and limpid, her diction pure and precise. The sweetness and grace of her lyrical melodies, the unforced naturalness of her style and syntax, a conversational idiom quickened by a delicate ear for song, set her as a poet at the opposite pole from Hopkins. And though she shares with him a delight in the world of nature, her response to its beauties is simple, and almost childlike, compared to his sense of the richness, complexity, variety, and 'instress' of the natural world. Yet her poetry is never in danger of over-sweetness, because her faith, like his, was a stern one, making high demands and calling for sacrifice; and, along with her sense of the beauty of the world, there went a deep sense of the pathos of its transience and of the unsatisfactoriness of this life. Stern with herself, and disillusioned with the world, Christina Rossetti combines grace and sweetness with an underlying strength. It is here that she touches Hopkins:

> *God strengthen me to bear myself;*
> *That heaviest weight of all to bear,*
> *Inalienable weight of care.*
>
> *All others are outside myself;*
> *I lock my door and bar them out,*
> *The turmoil, tedium, gad-about.*

I lock my door upon myself,
And bar them out; but who shall wall
Self from myself, most loathed of all?

If I could once lay down myself,
And start self-purged upon the race
That all must run! Death runs apace.

If I could set aside myself,
And start with lightened heart upon
The road by all men overgone!

God harden me against myself,
This coward with pathetic voice
Who craves for ease, and rest, and joys:

Myself, arch-traitor to myself;
My hollowest friend, my deadliest foe,
My clog whatever road I go.

Yet One there is can curb myself,
Can roll the strangling load from me,
Break off the yoke and set me free.

The heroic note that we miss in Victorian poetry generally is here, underlying the muted tone. It is present again in a handful of poems in which Emily Brontë attempted to render her vision of the divine and her sense of commitment to her 'God of Visions'. In these an extraordinary force of nature makes itself felt. Most of the masculine poets of her century seem, in comparison with her, soft feminine souls. The two poems known as 'The Visionary' ('Silent is the house; all are laid asleep') and 'The Prisoner' ('In the dungeon crypts idly did I stray') are now realized to be portions of a long poem headed, in Emily Brontë's transcription of 'Gondal Poems' in the British Museum, 'Julian M. and A. G. Rochelle'. Charlotte published the first three stanzas with two additional stanzas under the title 'The Visionary' in the handful

of Emily's poems added to *Wuthering Heights* in 1850. But Emily
had herself already lifted portions of this poem for publication in
the *Poems* of 1846, where fifteen stanzas (lines 13–44 and 65–92),
with an additional concluding stanza, appeared under the heading
'The Prisoner. A Fragment'. Whether the fourth and fifth stanzas
of 'The Visionary', which Charlotte added to the three opening
stanzas of the long poem in the Gondal manuscript, are her own
or not, does not affect the beauty of the poem as printed; nor
should we too easily assume that Charlotte understood her sister
less well than do modern students of her writings. The added
stanzas make sense of what is really unintelligible in the Gondal
poem: the cryptic third stanza, in which a girl locked up from her
lover and threatened by her cruel parents appears to be speaking.
But in the fourth stanza, where Emily began her own excerpt, the
speaker is a man, 'straying in dungeons', where he finds a beautiful, captive girl. The poem appears to make a completely fresh
start.

In Gondal and its inhabitants and its history, Emily Brontë
found not only a world of romantic passions, violent actions and
stern conflicts, but also a means of expressing the inexpressible. It
may be true that 'Last Lines' ('No coward soul is mine') was
spoken 'by a Gondalian facing a crisis incident to the Republican-
Royalist conflict', though Miss Ratchford, who tells us this, does
not tell us what 'evidence indicates' it. If true, it only means that,
through the rather tawdry and infantile romanticism of the Gondal stories, Emily Brontë found means to express an intense faith
and an unshakeable sense of the communion of the devoted soul
and its God. Whether it is a Gondal poem or not, this is a great
religious poem. In 'The Visionary' and 'The Prisoner', which are
unquestionably Gondal poems in origin, secular myths of power
are used: the girl threatened by her parents and kept from her
lover, and the prisoner in his cell. The girl is the standard heroine
of romantic fiction. The prisoner, doomed by tyrants to solitary
imprisonment, is one of the archetypal figures of the age that
opens with the symbolic act of the Fall of the Bastille. He appears
in Byron's *The Prisoner of Chillon*, and in Beethoven's *Fidelio*, in

the novels of Dickens, and in later Italian opera. Emily Brontë's force of passion, which burns through a certain banality of language and redeems what might otherwise be barrel-organ metres, finds in these stock romantic figures vehicles through which to express what can only be called mystical experience. Sometimes this theme occupies the whole poem; at other times it expresses itself in stanzas that arise in the midst of a conventionally romantic story, as in the celebrated stanzas from 'The Prisoner' which conflict so oddly with the image of the pale, beautiful, captive girl and the romantic happy ending of the manuscript poem:

Still, let my tyrants know, I am not doomed to wear
Year after year in gloom and desolate despair;
A messenger of Hope comes every night to me,
And offers, for short life, eternal liberty.

He comes with western winds, with evening's wandering airs,
With that clear dusk of heaven that brings the thickest stars;
Winds take a pensive tone, and stars a tender fire,
And visions rise and change that kill me with desire—

Desire for nothing known in my maturer years
When joy grew mad with awe at counting future tears;
When, if my spirit's sky was full of flashes warm,
I knew not whence they came, from sun or thunderstorm;

But first a hush of peace, a soundless calm descends;
The struggle of distress and fierce impatience ends;
Mute music soothes my breast—unuttered harmony
That I could never dream till earth was lost to me.

Then dawns the Invisible, the Unseen its truth reveals;
My outward sense is gone, my inward essence feels—
Its wings are almost free, its home, its harbour found;
Measuring the gulf it stoops and dares the final bound!

O dreadful is the check—intense the agony
When the ear begins to hear and the eye begins to see;
When the pulse begins to throb, the brain to think again,
The soul to feel the flesh and the flesh to feel the chain!

Yet I would lose no sting, would wish no torture less;
The more that anguish racks the earlier it will bless;
And robed in fires of Hell, or bright with heavenly shine,
If it but herald Death, the vision is divine![1]

In earlier ages the religious poet did not seem to be writing against the current of his age, but to be adapting to his special subject-matter the forms and styles of contemporary poetry, and to be writing in the spirit of its ideals. By the nineteenth century we are aware that the religious poet stands in some measure apart, supplying sometimes, as Hopkins, Christina Rossetti and Emily Brontë do, what contrasts with rather than reflects the prevailing attitudes and ideals of secular poetry. The two greatest poets in our language of this century, Yeats and Eliot, exemplify very well the limitations of the religious poet in an age in which conditions are in many ways 'unpropitious'. Yeats, although no poet has a greater sense of a spiritual reality underlying the show of things, refused to accept the fetters of religious commitment. In a set of poems under the title 'Vacillation', he inserted a little dialogue between the Soul and the Heart, and gave the Heart the last word:

> The Soul.   *Seek out reality, leave things that seem.*
> The Heart.   *What, be a singer born and lack a theme?*
> The Soul.   *Isaiah's coal, what more can man desire?*
> The Heart.   *Struck dumb in the simplicity of fire!*
> The Soul.   *Look on that fire, salvation walks within.*
> The Heart.   *What theme had Homer but original sin?*

And he ended by asserting

[1] I have kept the lighter manuscript punctuation, though taking the first line from the printed version.

Homer is my example and his unchristened heart.
The lion and the honey-comb, what has Scripture said?
So get you gone, Von Hügel, though with blessing on your head.

His 'unchristened heart' gives to Yeats's poetry a far wider range than Eliot enjoys; he has a boldness of imagination, a splendour of diction, a glory of speech that Eliot lacks. By his very eclecticism, his refusal of commitment, his imagination is freed to discover intimations of reality that enlarge our whole concept of the significance of our experience. But Eliot's deep sense of commitment, the persistence and integrity with which he endeavours to make sense and find meaning in what seem to him his most significant experiences, gives his poetry a special kind of intensity and a special immediacy that the richer and more various poetry of Yeats lacks. There are times and seasons when Eliot speaks to us and Yeats seems to be only speaking at us.

Eliot's achievement was to manage to express a rigorous acceptance of the tradition of Western Christianity in a language and through symbols that owe nothing to the traditional language and traditional symbols of the Church. The blend of an extreme individuality of language, a highly personal and yet not eccentric idiom; of an imagery that is also highly personal, yet is made of the stuff of ordinary experience, and is in no way exotic; and of a highly original formal inventiveness, with an extreme orthodoxy of belief is Eliot's distinctive achievement. He created for himself a language for rendering spiritual experience while accepting the interpretation of that experience of the Christian centuries. The most beautiful example in a small compass is *Marina*, a poem in which no single religious word is used. As the fourteenth-century poet employed the language of courtly love, and Emily Brontë took up the romantic figure of the prisoner, Eliot took up the myth of restoration from Shakespeare's last plays, plays which our age has found to be peculiarly significant. It is a symbolic poem, written in the idiom of our day, needing no interpretation, concerned with what is given, with effort and struggle, and with dying into life.

III

Seventeenth-century Religious Poetry

The seventeenth century, or at least the first half of it, is so great an age of religious poetry in England that it demands extended discussion. Not only is the greatest poet of the century, Milton, a religious poet; but there is hardly a single poet of stature who did not, on occasion, write religious verse, and there are some poets of high excellence who wrote virtually nothing else. There is a wealth of religious verse and also a great variety. All the different methods of treating the subject are found: the 'frontal assault', 'transferred classicism', 'humble sobriety', and the indirect approach, by way of parable. Almost all forms, in a century remarkable for the wide variety of forms it found congenial, are used: odes, hymns, cantatas, sonnets, songs, epistles, dialogues and answer poems, emblems and acrostics. Such diverse kinds as pastoral poetry and the majestic and hallowed forms of classical epic and classical tragedy are made vehicles for the expression of religious truth and religious experience.

Various reasons can be suggested why the seventeenth century in England provided such favourable conditions for the writing of religious poetry. There is first the stress on poetry as an art, and on the poem as something made and judged according to known canons of composition. The educational system rested very largely on the close analysis of literary texts, and on the art of composition and imitation of the ancients. Many poets saw it as their function to adorn their native tongue by creative imitation of the great poets of the past, and of poets in all tongues. This going to school, as it were, to the tradition of European poetry

[*171*]

from antiquity did not inhibit, but rather liberated, originality and individuality. Unconcerned with the idea that a poet expresses his personality, and concerned instead with the aim of giving fitting treatment in an appropriate form to a chosen subject, the poets of the seventeenth century reveal strongly individual personalities and develop strongly individual styles. The tradition they inherited was so rich and so diverse that it inspired and did not restrict. The divine poet, who wished to make Apollo serve Christ, was doing the same thing as many of his secular contemporaries were doing: adapting forms and styles to a chosen subject-matter. This may go some way to explain why the religious poetry of the period has such security of tone, such an absence of strained feeling.

It does not explain why the sixteenth century, which equally believed in imitation and desired to baptize the Muse, is so barren of good religious poetry while the seventeenth century is so rich. The difference here can be explained as a reflection of the different religious climate of the two periods. The poets of the seventeenth century harvested the fruits of the religious revolution and the bitter religious conflicts of the sixteenth century. They are the heirs of the Reformation in its two aspects: the Protestant Reformation and the Counter-Reformation. In England, the Elizabethan settlement allowed a fine religious eclecticism, hardly paralleled in any other country. Whatever one may think of the theory of the 'via media', or of the 'bridge church' or of the 'three branches', or any other attempt to define the position of the Church of England, Elizabeth's ambiguous and temporizing settlement, which settled so little, had as one of its results the spiritual freedom of the seventeenth-century poets. They draw happily and unselfconsciously on Roman Catholic works of devotion and piety ('taking the grain and leaving the chaff' to use their language), while drawing also on the great Protestant source of inspiration, the words of Scripture, and on the insights of the early Fathers, and revealing to the full the 'inwardness' that is the mark of Protestant devotion. This devout eclecticism has made the poets of the earlier seventeenth century loved and valued by

Christians of all denominations. And the centrality of their out-
look, along with the fineness of their art, has made them admired
and loved by many who are not Christians and who normally find
religious poetry repellent. Such persons will nearly always make
an exception for George Herbert.

It is necessary to stress the wealth and variety of the religious
poetry of the century because, just as to many people medieval
religious poetry means the carol, so to many people religious
poetry in the seventeenth century means the religious lyric, the
religious poems of the so-called metaphysical poets. These
strikingly negate Johnson's statement that 'contemplative piety,
or the intercourse between God and the human soul, cannot be
"poetical"', and strikingly demonstrate individuality of temper
and style within the bounds of what we still have to call the
"metaphysical" manner.[1] This individuality appears even more
striking when we remember that many of these poets were closely
linked by personal admiration, if not by friendship. The relation
of Donne to Herbert has, I think, been exaggerated. Donne was
a friend of Edward Herbert, George's much older brother, and of
their mother, Magdalen Herbert. The only surviving link between George Herbert and Donne is the verses they exchanged
on Donne's emblematic seal of Christ on the Anchor. I have
given elsewhere reasons for doubting Walton's statement that
George Herbert was one of those to whom Donne sent a dying
gift of one of these seals.[2] Donne was twenty years Herbert's
senior and his poems were not published until after Herbert's
death. Though it is very probable he saw them in manuscript,
there are very few even possible borrowings from Donne in
Herbert's poetry and none that are unquestionable. We cannot
say with any certainty that Herbert was familiar with Donne's
Divine Poems. But both Crashaw and Vaughan regarded them-

---

[1] The term is universally admitted to be unsatisfactory; but so are
the various terms that have been suggested to replace it. The fact that
so many attempts have been made shows that a term is needed, and it
seems best to make do with the established one.

[2] See Appendix G to my edition of *The Divine Poems of John Donne*
(1952).

selves as Herbert's followers in sacred poetry. Crashaw called his volume *Steps to the Temple*, humbly suggesting its relation to Herbert's volume, *The Temple*, and Vaughan, in the preface to *Silex Scintillans*, declared himself to be Herbert's convert, and proved it by wholesale imitation and borrowing. He must have known *The Temple* almost by heart. Yet nobody who is familiar with the work of these three poets would have any difficulty in assigning a poem by one of them to its true author.

Recent scholarship has found further links between these poets. Rosemond Tuve, whose early death all students of the period must mourn, in her *A Reading of George Herbert* (1952), and I, myself, in my edition of Donne's *Divine Poems* in the same year, attempted to show how much of the 'wit' of Donne and Herbert is traditional. The paradoxes, twistings of Scripture, borrowings from the liturgy, allegorical interpretations, the use of typology, all these things reach back through centuries of Scriptural commentary and liturgical use to the early Fathers, and indeed to the New Testament itself. Professor Louis Martz, working independently, came to the same conclusion as I had reached in studying Donne's 'Holy Sonnets': that the practice of formal meditation, as systematized in the sixteenth century, strongly influenced the themes and the forms of the religious lyric of the seventeenth. I was confining myself to Donne: Professor Martz in *The Poetry of Meditation* (1954) took a wider theme and showed the influence of the religious exercise of meditation, in varying ways and to varying degrees, on all the religious poets of the century. Like all pioneers, Professor Martz perhaps overstated his case, and did not sufficiently allow for the fact that the same pattern, of setting a theme, developing it by points, and coming to a conclusion, is found in the love poets as well as the religious poets, and is the result of the intellectuality that is characteristic of the seventeenth century and appears in other arts beside poetry. But he made abundantly clear how much the characteristic spirituality of the Counter-Reformation, embodied in the *Spiritual Exercises* of St. Ignatius Loyola, and flowering in a rather different form later in the 'devout humanism' of France, developed fully by St. Francis de Sales, is reflected in English poetry. These poets are thus linked personally; linked by being brought up in a common religious tradition, for Crashaw, although he became a Roman Catholic, was the son of a noted Puritan preacher and must, in his formative years, have been exposed like the others to the Protestant stress on the language of the Bible, and to the language of the Book of Common Prayer; and they are linked by their readiness to assimilate Continental influences. Yet the more scholarship establishes links, the more original and independent they seem. In the religious lyrics of the metaphysicals, even more than in their love poetry (always excepting Donne) we are aware that this style of writing encourages an individual tone and an individual excellence. The strength of the appeal of the poetry of this age lies in its power to give us the best of both worlds: classic themes treated with personal independence; a poetry of personal response and personal reflection on common situations and common experience.

Professor Martz rightly placed the metaphysical religious lyric in its proper temporal and spatial setting in the Europe of the sixteenth and seventeenth centuries. He emphasized the Continental influences on English religious thought, and piety, and poetry, and also made clear the relation and the difference between the temper of the sixteenth century and the temper of the later Middle Ages. This is something that goes beyond and is more important than the differences between Catholics and Protestants. It unites them and makes their quarrels have the bitterness of quarrels between brothers. In the later Middle Ages—the movement of thought and feeling is clear by the end of the fourteenth century—there is a falling apart of what are united in the thirteenth century: theology and devotion. The characteristic piety of the fourteenth and fifteenth centuries is affectionate, and takes the form of an intense devotion to the Humanity of Christ and his Mother. The sense of the awfulness of the Godhead veiled in flesh, and the marvel of the woman chosen to be the tabernacle of Deity, is obscured by the pathos of the babe born in a stable and the sweetness of the maiden-mother who rocks him in her arms and sings

him to sleep. The suffering Saviour, scourged, mocked, crowned
with thorns, falling beneath the load of the Cross, dying in agony,
to be taken down into the arms of his nearly swooning mother,
to be laid exhausted and drained of blood in the tomb, obsessed
the imaginations of painters and sculptors. These images replaced
the *Christus Victor* and *Christus Rex*, the strong Son of God. The
artists were following the trend of the preachers and the movements of popular devotion. The meditations on the life of Christ,
ascribed to St. Bonaventura, set the model for countless imitations,
which expanded with concrete and painful imaginative detail
the bare Gospel narratives. Such meditations lie behind the mystery plays (which borrow from them details such as how Christ
was actually nailed to the Cross), and the religious lyrics of the
later Middle Ages. They are embodied in visual form in paintings
and sculptures all over Europe. The mother and her babe, the
mother and her dying or dead son, become supreme embodi-
ments of loving and suffering humanity. When we speak of
medieval religious feeling, or medieval art, it is this late medieval
presentation of Christ in his Humanity that we usually mean, the
fruit of the Franciscan devotion to the Babe of Bethlehem and the
Man of Sorrows.

These tender and moving images replaced earlier and more
majestic conceptions, such as we find in early Christian mosaics,
in painters of the Byzantine tradition, and in many primitives. In
place of the mother lulling her child and mourning the hard fate
that he is to suffer, the artists present the solemn Virgin, seated
erect on her royal, cushioned throne, staring before her, like some
awful priestess. Her lap is a throne on which the divine infant,
dressed as an infant priest, sits; his hand is raised in blessing. Instead of a figure hanging from its arms, with thorn-crowned,
drooping head, the feet crossed and nailed through, the knees bent
sideways with the weight of the body dragging on the nails, the
body naked and emaciated, the ribs standing out and blood
streaming from its wounds, earlier artists showed a white-robed
and crowned figure, standing on a ledge with feet firmly placed
side by side, his arms spread out in power and blessing, looking

out over the world he has redeemed in calm majesty, reigning from the tree. These earlier representations are symbols charged with intellectual meaning. They are intended to arouse religious awe, not to evoke tender, affectionate compassion and warm feeling.

The divorce between theology and devotion is one of the diseases that afflicted Christendom in the later Middle Ages. Theology came to seem mere barren speculation, the arid late scholasticism against which the humanists rail. Devotion degenerated into superstition. Catholics and Protestants have in common a reaction against a purely affectionate piety, divorced from intellectual and theological conceptions. Among Protestants this takes the form of an overwhelming re-emphasis on the Majesty of God, so that in Protestant piety devotion to the Person of Christ in his Humanity is very rare. Christ the Redeemer, whose righteousness is the righteousness of his elect, who reigns in heaven, dominates the Protestant religious consciousness, with the indwelling Spirit who gives assurance of salvation. Among Catholics, the reaction takes the form of attempting to infuse the affectionate piety of the Middle Ages with intellectual and theological meaning, to make such time-honoured exercises as the religious meditation more than a mode of arousing the affections and thus stimulating the will to love, by deepening understanding before arousing the will. The method of meditation with the three powers of the mind, memory, understanding and will, is a development and systematization of the freer and more discursive medieval meditation, in which the memory, or imagination, disported itself much more at liberty. Memory, or imagination's task was to provide the *compositio loci*, by vividly recalling, or rather creating in the imagination, a scene or situation. Understanding was then to discover points of significance; and lastly the Will was to make appropriate and definite resolves, expressing its affection and its resolves in the final colloquy. The *Spiritual Exercises* of Ignatius Loyola of 1548 set a pattern for many works of piety in which this method of bringing all the powers of the mind into play in a concentrated exercise spread all over Europe.

The method corresponds very well to Donne's description of how a poem is made:

> In all Metricall compositions, of which kinde the booke of Psalmes is, the force of the whole piece, is for the most part left to the shutting up; the whole frame of the Poem is a beating out of a piece of gold, but the last clause is as the impression of a stamp, and that it is that makes it currant.[1]

The subject proposed for the poem, the scene or situation called up for meditation, are like the unworked lump of gold. The points made in the poem's argument, or in the meditation, are the beating-out of the gold; and the stamp is the conclusion to which the poem's argument tends, or the colloquy and resolves with which the meditation closes.

The stress, therefore, in seventeenth-century religious poetry is rather different from the medieval stress on the dogma, the mystery, the fact of faith. It is either on the individual soul's attempt to lay hold on and apprehend the mystery; or else, when the theme is more general and the poem does not express an individual devotion, it is on the significances and the subtleties rather than on the simplicities of doctrine. Professor Tuve spent many pages in showing how traditional Herbert's long poem 'The Sacrifice' was. She demonstrated fully that it rests upon liturgical material, the 'Reproaches', and that its paradoxes, and allegorizations, and wealth of typological allusions are from the common stock of Christian tradition through the ages. But if we set 'The Sacrifice' against the late fifteenth-century poem 'Woefully arrayed', wrongly attributed to Skelton, we can see at once that there is a world of difference between them, which justifies us in calling Herbert's poem a 'witty poem'. We would never dream of calling 'Woefully arrayed' witty. 'Woefully arrayed' makes one point and one point only, and it makes it very movingly:

> *Woefully arrayed,*
> *My blode, man, for thee ran,*

---

[1] *Sermons*, edited G. R. Potter and Evelyn M. Simpson (1953–62), VI, p. 41.

It may not be naid,
My body blo and wan,
Woefully arrayed.

The poem expands this one theme:

What myght I suffer more
Than I have suffered, man, for thee?

Compared with this simple, sorrowful insistence on the pain of
the Cross, Herbert's poem is highly sophisticated. It is packed
with Biblical theology and Biblical reference, and constantly
stresses a theological point: the irony of the voluntary sacrifice of
Christ. It is by his power that his enemies are given power to
destroy him:

They use that power against me, which I gave.

Herbert's poem aims at a completeness of theological statement
that is beyond the scope or desire of the medieval poet. Something
has happened to the characteristic medieval form of the plaint of
Christ from the Cross. It has ceased to be a direct appeal: 'See,
man, what I suffer for thee. Love me, for I have loved thee.' It
has become less poignant, less humanly moving; it is more mysterious, more impressive. As Christ speaks, he reveals not simply
the love for man that made him endure a shameful and agonizing
death, but the whole economy of salvation. Herbert includes in
his poem the complete narrative of the Passion. He implies the
whole scheme that began with Adam's eating of the apple, and
included the calling of Abraham, the rescue of Israel from
Pharaoh's yoke, the election of David as King, and issues finally
in the sacrament of the Body and Blood:

Nay, after death their spite shall further go;
For they will pierce my side, I full well know;
That as sinne came, so Sacraments might flow:
Was ever grief like mine?

The same retreat from the actualities of the human life and

death of Christ appears in the treatment of that other favourite theme of medieval poets, the Nativity. Milton's 'Ode on the Morning of Christ's Nativity' stands in a class apart because of its large Miltonic scope and the exquisite elaboration of its art. All the same, it is through and through of its century. The Babe of Bethlehem is here the infant God who, like a greater Hercules, 'to shew his Godhead true'

Can in his swadling bands controul the damned crew.

The hymn is designed like a huge seventeenth-century painting, intellectually organized around its centre, the point from which it begins and to which it returns at the close: the 'Courtly Stable', around which

Bright-harnest Angels sit in order serviceable.

In the distance the procession of the Magi can be seen, hastening down a winding road. Allegorical figures are descending from clouds above. On one side the Kings of the earth sit, with their weapons of war hung up behind them as trophies. In contrast to them are the shepherds who sit 'simply chatting in a rustick row'. Within a globe of light the celestial choir appears. In contrast again, in glooming light and shade the pagan gods retreat discomforted. The contrasts of light and darkness, the sensationalism with which the unhallowed rites of paganism are treated, the light striking down upon their dark, unholy ceremonies and touching more tenderly the nymphs who 'in twilight shade of tangled thickets mourn', remind us of the passion for effects of light and darkness and the fondness for making light strike downwards of Caravaggio and his followers in the *seicento*. Milton's Ode is a splendid composition, including in its range of reference the original Creation, the giving of the Law on Sinai, and the end of all things when

The dreadfull Judge in middle Air shall spread his throne.

And if we turn from Milton's classical ode to a poem that is sometimes contrasted with it, as having the warmth and human tenderness of the Catholic tradition which the Protestant Milton is thought to lack, Crashaw's 'Hymn of the Nativity', we are still very remote from the medieval shepherds offering their 'bob of cherries' or playing on their pipes. Crashaw's poem is an elaborate cantata. His shepherds are not the naïve peasants of the Portail Royal at Chartres, or the hard-working experts on lambing of the English mystery plays, and have ideas and gifts beyond the scope of jolly Wat the good herdsboy. They are well instructed theologians, with a gift for paradox and oxymoron, exceedingly 'well read in their simplicity'. They have not come to see Jesus laughing or weeping on his mother's knee. They have 'met love's Noon in Nature's night'. They are Thyrsis and Tityrus, prepared to sing in solo or ensemble, as unlike the working shepherds of medieval sculptors, painters and dramatists as Donatello's boy David in the Bargello is unlike any Tuscan shepherd-boy of any age. They are capable of such splendid flights of intellectual apprehension as

> *The Phoenix builds the Phoenix nest.*
> *Love's architecture is his own.*

The traditions of classical pastoral, developments in sacred music, and the effort of theologians to make precise the meaning of the Incarnation lie behind Crashaw's poem and are summed in the final chorus of the shepherds:

> *Welcome all wonders in one sight!*
> *Eternity shut in a span!*
> *Summer in winter, day in night,*
> *Heaven in earth, and God in man.*
> *Great little one! whose all-embracing birth*
> *Lifts earth to heaven, stoops heaven to earth.*

These two poems are public poems, celebrations of the 'mystery of love' in seventeenth-century terms. The poet employs all the resources of his art and all the powers of his mind to render apprehensible to the imagination of his readers that central moment in human history when God became Man. But equally in the poems of private and personal devotion there is intellectual organization and a refined, even sophisticated, art. When man in

meditation, prayer, thanksgiving, or penitence speaks to his
Saviour, or attempts to render in parable, or allegory, how his
God has dealt with him, he does so in poems controlled by a line
of argument, illuminated by those flashes of intellectual insight
that we call 'wit', with a propriety of diction so refined that we
hardly realize its elegance, and in a great variety of stanza forms,
many of considerable difficulty. It is often said that the twin
glories of the early seventeenth century are the love lyric and the
religious lyric; and it is true that this is our great age of love poetry
as well as of religious poetry. As in the fourteenth century the
religious poets adopted the language and the conventions of
courtly love and saw the Virgin as the Lady of troubador convention and Christ as the Knight-Lover, wooing the soul of man
and offering the service of love, so the religious poets of the
seventeenth century deliberately attempted to rival the love-poets.
According to Walton, Herbert wrote, 'in the first year of his going
to Cambridge', reproving the 'vanity of those many Love poems,
that are daily writ and consecrated to *Venus*', and bewailing 'that
so few are writ, that look towards God and Heaven':

> *Doth Poetry*
> *Wear* Venus *Livery? only serve her turn?*
> *Why are not* Sonnets *made of thee? and layes*
> *Upon thine Altar burnt? Cannot thy love*
> *Heighten a spirit to sound out thy praise*
> *As well as any she? Cannot thy* Dove
> *Out-strip their* Cupid *easily in flight?*

And in the poem 'Dullness', in *The Temple*, he made the same
comparison:

> *The wanton lover in a curious strain*
>   *Can praise his fairest fair;*
> *And with quaint metaphors her curled hair*
>   *Curl o're again.*

> *Thou art my lovelinesse, my life, my light,*
>   *Beautie alone to me:*

> *Thy bloudy death and undeserved, makes thee*
> *Pure red and white.*

But, as Professor Tuve pointed out in a brilliant paper on 'George Herbert and *Caritas*',[1] if we are going to speak of the religious poems of the seventeenth century as love poems addressed to God, they must be recognized to be love poems of a very curious kind. For, whereas in most love poetry it is the wooer who speaks and pleads with his mistress to reward his loving service and love him in return, here the speaker is not pleading to be loved and protesting his own loyalty and service. He is, and has been, and knows that he is, and has been, loved. The faithfulness, and the constancy, and the suffering for love's sake are all on the other side. His plea is to be made worthy of such a love and to be given grace to love in some measure in return. The seventeenth-century poet rarely attempts to follow the medieval poets in presenting the love of God directly in the wooing of man's soul. He prefers to present the wooed rather than the wooer; and the wooed is often reluctant and unwilling and ungracious. If Herbert allows God to speak in his poems, apart from 'The Sacrifice', which is *sui generis* among his poems, it is in dialogue, as in the poem so called which begins and ends with the soul speaking. Here Herbert comes near to the medieval plea of Christ to man; but there is a world of difference between the directness of the appeal of the wounded Servant of Love in '*Quia Amore Langueo*', and the delicate stress in Herbert's dialogue on the soul's reluctance, its egotistic unwillingness to be accepted and remade:

> *Sweetest Saviour, if my soul*
> *Were but worth the having,*
> *Quickly should I then controll*
> *Any thought of waving.*
> *But when all my care and pains*
> *Cannot give the name of gains*
> *To thy wretch so full of stains,*
> *What delight or hope remains?*

[1] *Journal of the Warburg and Courtauld Institutes*, Vol. XXII (1959).

What, Child, is the ballance thine,
   Thine the poise and measure?
If I say, Thou shalt be mine;
   Finger not my treasure.
What the gains in having thee
Do amount to, onely he,
Who for man was sold, can see;
That transferr'd th'accounts to me.

But as I can see no merit,
   Leading to this favour:
So the way to fit me for it
   Is beyond my savour.
As the reason then is thine;
So the way is none of mine:
I disclaim the whole designe:
Sinne disclaims and I resigne.

That is all, if that I could
   Get without repining;
And my clay, my creature, would
   Follow my resigning:
That as I did freely part
With my glorie and desert,
Left all joyes to feel all smart——
   Ah! no more: thou break'st my heart.

This is, as no medieval poem is, a 'witty' poem. It turns on the
Saviour's quick acceptance and translation of the sinner's word
'resign'. It is also, as no medieval poems is, an attempt to present
what Johnson called 'the intercourse between God and a human
soul'; and further, although it would be naïve to call that soul
'George Herbert' *tout court*, it has all the characteristics of Herbert's poetical personality, courtesy, refinement, a certain diffi-
dence, and a proneness to discouragement, along with a bedrock
of firm assurance:

As when th'heart sayes (sighing to be approved)
O, could I love! *and stops: God writeth,* Loved.

Usually, when God speaks in Herbert's poems, the dialogue takes place in the framework of an imagined situation, in which the divine initiative is shown anticipating the need, and overcoming the weakness of man, and making sufficient his insufficiency. In the parabolic sonnet 'Redemption', the discontented tenant has been anticipated by the action of the 'rich Lord', who has already left his 'manor' before the tenant decides to go and see him. When, having wrongly looked for him in 'cities, theatres, gardens, parks and courts', he at last finds him, he does not have to make his request. The Lord knows his need and grants his suit as soon as their eyes meet:

> *At length I heard a ragged noise and mirth*
> *Of theeves and murderers: there I him espied,*
> *Who straight,* Your suit is granted, *said & died.*

In the famous and beautiful poem 'Love', under the similitude of a host welcoming a hot, weary and dirty traveller, Herbert glances at the Eucharistic feast on earth and the feast of Heaven, where 'Christ shall the banquet spread with his own royal hand.' The language used is wholly appropriate to the ordinariness of the imagined situation: a kind host making an embarrassed and shame-faced guest welcome, overcoming by natural courtesy the un-happiness of someone who feels 'I really am too filthy to come in.' The easy, idiomatic style, with its abundance of monosyllables, its supremely natural rhymes, holds a colloquy between Christ and the soul even more delicate than that in 'Dialogue'. Love makes nothing of sufferings endured, and puts aside the contrition of the sinner and his desire to take punishment with a reference to what is over and done with: the 'blame' has been borne. And, finally, the soul's reluctance is overcome by the host's insistence that he must not leave the 'meat' prepared untasted. It is almost as if the sinner does his Lord a favour in accepting what has been done for him and what is offered.

[*185*]

But it is rare to find in the seventeenth century either a direct appeal of God to the soul, or dialogues, whether undisguised or disguised as little dramas. In the great majority of religious lyrics the centre is man, shown in prayer, or meditation, or wrestling with temptation. These are poems much concerned with what Aldous Huxley called 'inner weather'. Donne and Herbert are both masters of introspection, and Vaughan has a snail-horn sensitiveness to the movements of the spirit and to changes in the climate of the soul. In the seventeenth century we first find poems of spiritual dereliction, of doubt, self-disgust, and near despair. These poets are aware of painful weariness of spirit, and are willing to express it, as well as paying tribute to unexpected and unaccountable visitations of joy. As C. S. Lewis said, far from suggesting to us that they are saying what they feel they ought to say rather than what they really feel, the religious poets of the seventeenth century give an impression of remarkable truth of feeling. It would be odious to suggest that this was because they were more 'sincere' in their religion than religious poets of later ages, and to attempt to equate their success in rendering in verse the ups and downs of the spiritual life with a deeper spiritual experience or a more firmly grounded faith. But a very real difference in tone can be felt if we compare a sonnet by Hopkins and a poem by Herbert on the same theme, spiritual desolation.

I wake and feel the fell of dark, not day
What hours, O what black hoürs we have spent
This night! what sight you, heart, saw; ways you went!
And more must, in yet longer light's delay.
    With witness I speak this. But where I say
Hours I mean years, mean life. And my lament
Is cries countless, cries like dead letters sent
To dearest him that lives alas! away.

    I am gall, I am heartburn. God's most deep decree
Bitter would have me taste: my taste was me;
Bones built in me, flesh filled, blood brimmed the curse.

[*186*]

Self-yeast of spirit a dull dough sours. I see
The lost are like this, and their scourge to be
As I am mine, their sweating selves; but worse.

Moving and impressive as this sonnet is, there is a disquieting
sense of indulgence in self-disgust, and of exaggeration in the
stress on 'hours', 'hoürs', 'Hours I mean years, mean life'. And, as
often in Hopkins, there is an uneasy alternation between a worn
romantic diction—'ways you went' or 'blood brimmed the curse',
and a deliberately prosaic. The poem, for all its depth of feeling
and the exactness of so much of its phrasing, has a tone of con-
trivance, of the factitious. Perhaps it is rather too much to ask
that a poem on spiritual dereliction should sound 'natural'; but
should it sound melodramatic, or so deeply self-absorbed?

Herbert's 'Denial', on the other hand, does not aim at convincing the reader of the depth and force of the writer's feelings.
Herbert has a support in the general temper and artistic ideals of
his period that Hopkins lacks, and this enables him to approach
his subject with confidence.

When my devotions could not pierce
Thy silent eares;
Then was my heart broken, as was my verse:
My breast was full of fears
And disorder:

My bent thoughts, like a brittle bow,
Did fly asunder:
Each took his way; some would to pleasures go,
Some to the warres and thunder
Of alarms.

As good go any where, they say,
As to benumme
Both knees and heart, in crying night and day,
Come, come, my God, O come,
But no hearing.

[*187*]

O that thou shouldst give dust a tongue
To crie to thee,
And then not heare it crying! all day long
My heart was in my knee,
But no hearing.

Therefore my soul lay out of sight,
Untun'd, unstrung:
My feeble spirit, unable to look right,
Like a nipt blossome, hung
Discontented.

O cheer and tune my heartlesse breast,
Deferre no time;
That so thy favours granting my request,
They and my mind may chime,
And mend my ryme.

This poem is, in fact, far more artificial, or artful, than Hopkins's sonnet; yet it sounds far more natural. Each verse, until the last, ends with a line that does not rhyme; the stanza pattern is 'disordered'. It is only in the final verse that we see the analogy between the discord between his mind and his God and the discords of his poem, when, by the poem's last word, our ear is at last gratified by the 'chime' of 'ryme'. Herbert carefully distances his pain from us by speaking of it in the past tense; whereas Hopkins is attempting to render overwhelming personal experience and feeling at the moment when it overwhelms him. Yet the personal pain and the personal feeling in Herbert's poem seems to be rendered with extreme truthfulness; and his reproach to the God who gives men power to pray and then seems deaf to their prayers is more poignant than Hopkins's ascription of his misery to 'God's most deep decree'. Herbert's poem has two themes and they support each other. It is concerned with spiritual desolation, incapacity to pray, and with inability to write a poem. By thus seeing himself simultaneously as the soul abandoned to itself and the poet unable to achieve a poem, Herbert escapes the dilemma of the religious poet who aims at presenting actual spiritual experience in verse. There is, as Johnson rightly saw, a conflict between poetry, which aims at the highest possible articulateness, and prayer, which at its most intense passes into silence. And, at the opposite pole of spiritual experience, the sense of desolation and utter failure, of dereliction, sorts ill with the satisfaction of creating a poem. Herbert is not attempting to present us with a picture of his soul in its hour of despair. He comes before us as a man writing a poem. The mere fact that he is writing it shows that the hours of impotent misery have passed; the dayspring is returning after hours of darkness and confused turmoil of mind. Now that he is writing, even though his verse is 'disordered' and his rhymes unmended, we know, by implication, that his prayer was not really unheard. Herbert's very characteristic, preferred use of the past tense in those poems which treat of painful, personal experience is more than a mere desire to show God as always the victor, putting down the last trump to win the rubber. It is a recognition of the nature of his subject. Intense spiritual experience, like intense physical experience, cannot be rendered directly, and Herbert, by describing it as it was, rather than by trying to render it as it is, can keep that tone of 'humble sobriety' that convinces us of the truth of what he tells us.

It may be complained that Hopkins should not be set against Herbert, whose style and temper are so different, and that the true parallel to his 'terrible sonnets' is to be found in the 'Holy Sonnets' of Donne. That is true. Donne's sonnets have the dramatic immediacy of the present tense which Herbert, on the whole, tends to avoid, and some find them over-dramatic and too self-concerned. But even in the 'Holy Sonnets' there is a range of theological reference, a logic of thought as well as of feeling, and a width of reference in the imagery that universalizes the feeling; and almost all work towards a fine generality at the close. They are not claustrophobic, for all their intensity of personal feeling.

Many of the most beautiful of the religious lyrics of the century are autobiographical, or arise out of particular circumstances, whether actual or imagined. In the religious poetry we most find that sense of a particular place and time that we normally associate with romantic poetry. Donne writes on what he thinks to be his death-bed, 'tuning his intrument' before he is summoned to become God's music in heaven, or composes, 'at the sea-side' as one manuscript has it, his 'Hymn to Christ', a poem that arises out of his circumstances: newly widowed and about to go overseas to face a dangerous journey and travel through countries where he knows he has enemies. Or, he meditates as he rides westward one Good Friday on the fact that he appears to be turning his back on his crucified Saviour. Herbert, looking in his glass, sees his whitening hair and recognizes the sign of his failing powers; or finds after a night of heaviness that joy has unexpectedly returned in the morning. Vaughan sits at midnight thinking of departed friends, or walks out on a spring morning, or finds food for meditation in an evening shower that falls after a long misty morning in which damp air steamed up from the lake. Some of these situations are imagined, 'compositions of place' from which a meditation unfolds itself, as when Donne in his 'Holy Sonnets' imagines himself struck by a fatal illness, or on his death-bed, or at the moment when the angels blow the Last Trump. Others have the stamp of a particular occasion, such as 'Good Friday: Riding Westward', which begins as a discursive meditation, develops with mounting tension to the sudden apostrophe

> *and thou lookst towards mee,*
> *O Saviour, as thou hangst upon the tree,*

and ends with humility and penitence. This poem is essentially a dramatic monologue, not least in the sense it gives that a second person is present, though silent. As the poem proceeds we become conscious of the figure whose eyes the speaker feels are following him as he rides away towards the west. There is the same dramatic development, the development of thought and feeling to a conclusion, as distinguishes the finest of Donne's elegies and lyrics.

In Donne we have the one great poet of the century, with the possible exception of Marvell, who excelled in both love poetry and religious verse. He is, therefore, a key witness to the limitations that the writing of religious verse lays upon the poet.

Donne's imagination in his love poetry ranges freely and at will. Its truth is a truth of feeling, playing over personal experience and human experience generally. The poems are not dependent on any ideals, ethical or social, outside themselves. Each creates its own moral climate. Their language is equally all their own. Donne owes almost nothing to the words and phrases of other poets in his own or any other language. In his divine poetry, on the other hand, feeling and thought are judged by a standard that is always implied and often stated: the subject is not only what I feel, but what I ought, or ought not, to feel. And as a Christian, Donne cannot avoid using the language of the Bible and of the worship of the Church. Living in an age in which it could be said that 'the truest poetry is the most feigning', Donne apologized, as well he might, for the feebleness of his poem on the Marquis of Hamilton, on the ground that its subject, the reward of the saints in heaven, 'had so much truth, as it defeats all Poetry'. It was, he said, a subject for a sermon rather than for a poem. Donne's religious poetry develops out of his moral poetry, his Satires and the more serious and thoughtful of his Verse-Letters, more than out of his love poetry. The image of Christ the Lover is not dominant in his religious poetry, any more than in his Sermons. His twin themes are Judgment and Mercy, and his religious poetry is dominated by the image of Christ the Saviour, redeeming man from sin and death. We miss in the *Divine Poems* the élan of the *Songs and Sonnets*, their splendid hyperboles, the note of personal discovery, the virtuosity in the handling of argument, and the brilliance in the invention and manipulation of stanza forms. But if there is loss, there is also gain. The 'Holy Sonnets' and the three late Hymns have an intensity of their own. They express what is never expressed in Donne's love poetry: a sense of human need. And here, as also in 'A Litany', in place of a daring that explores to its limits a single experience and finds all value in that, there is an attempt, not less moving, if less exciting, to express a serious recognition of human weakness, and a desire for the 'evennesse' that peace of conscience brings. I do not suppose that anyone, allowed to choose only five poems by Donne for inclusion in an anthology of English poetry, would not choose as one of their

five the 'Hymn to God the Father', written in his grave illness of
1623. This has all the mastery of stanza form, the completeness of
statement, coming with a twist of the refrain to its conclusion, the
skill in the use of natural speech rhythms and of natural rhyme
that distinguish Donne's love poems. By a witty turn, the play
on his own name signs the poem at the close. But it has a sobriety
that we do not normally associate with Donne, and a muted
melody instead of the soaring tone of his love poetry. He goes
here, in Eliot's words, 'by a way wherein there is no ecstasy',
trusting not in his own power but in the promise to Abraham, the
father of the faithful. This poem does not render the truth of a
moment of passionate experience: it sums a life and has a painful
honesty.

> *Wilt thou forgive that sinne where I begunne,*
>   *Which is my sin, though it were done before?*
> *Wilt though forgive those sinnes through which I runne,*
>   *And doe them still: though still I doe deplore?*
>   *When thou hast done, thou hast not done,*
>   *For, I have more.*
>
> *Wilt thou forgive that sinne by which I wonne*
>   *Others to sinne? and made my sinne their doore?*
> *Wilt thou forgive that sinne which I did shunne*
>   *A yeare, or two: but wallowed in, a score?*
>   *When thou hast done, thou hast not done,*
>   *For, I have more.*
>
> *I have a sinne of feare, that when I have spunne*
>   *My last thred, I shall perish on the shore;*
> *Sweare by thy selfe, that at my death thy Sunne*
>   *Shall shine as it shines now, and heretofore;*
>   *And, having done that, Thou has done,*
>   *I have no more.*

Three things make the religious poetry of the seventeenth
century so satisfying to the lover of poetry, whatever his beliefs.
There is first the frank reliance of the poets on art. Their poems
are made poems, not effusions of feeling. Religion, in the sense
in which I have used it in my definition, implies obligation,

acceptance, a sense of entering into a fellowship of believers, living and dead, and a desire to escape or transcend the self. The feeling that the subject is greater than the treatment, and the poem more important than the poet goes well with the religious sense of the importance of the given. The poet and the believer are in accord. Secondly, the poetry of this period has a strongly intellectual bias. Its religious poetry, though full of feeling, emotion, strength of devotion and personal faith, is laced by, and built upon, a scheme of thought, and a universe of discourse that is not the poet's own invention, but has the toughness of systems that have been debated and argued over for centuries. And lastly, I would point to the unembarrassed boldness and naturalness with which these poets approach their subject, and the freedom with which they bring the experiences of daily life, their experience of art, their native powers of mind, their skill in argument and their wit, to play over religious doctrine, religious experience and religious imperatives. This is seen in their confident use of language. They are free of any taint of pious cant and of conventional religious diction. They use the language of educated men appropriately adapted to their subject and treatment: splendid and resourceful, as in Milton and Crashaw, when celebration is demanded, direct and nervous in the lyrics of personal devotion. Coleridge was surely right when he saw in the religious lyrics of the seventeenth century the achievement of a middle style unsurpassed for purity, strength and grace.

But admiration for the religious poets of the seventeenth century needs to be tempered. It was a period singularly propitious for the writing of religious poetry, and it makes the discussion of whether religious poetry is or is not minor poetry seem, as I think it is, rather a waste of time. The same debate could be held over love poetry, which is rare in some ages, and which many of our greatest poets have not attempted or have failed in. For all this, there are themes beyond the power of the poets of the seventeenth century, religious insights and modes of expressing them that are outside their range. For all the beauty of the poetry of natural description and the natural images in the religious poetry of Vaughan and Traherne, and Marvell, the world of nature remains for them still the 'book of the creatures' in which man finds lessons. The great romantic insight into a universe independent of man and man's needs, of which man is not Lord and Master, is taken up in the poetry of Hopkins, as he takes up the romantic theme of revolt against urban life. If, when we set Hopkins against Herbert and Vaughan, we feel some things have been lost, others have been gained. Apart from Milton and Traherne, whose imaginations were aroused by the conception of the infinity of the universe, the religious poets of the seventeenth century remain imaginatively bound to the conception of the universe expressed by Herbert in his poem 'Man', summed in the words 'Then how are all things neat!' No seventeenth-century poet could have conceived or written such poems as 'Pied Beauty', 'Hurrahing in Harvest', or 'God's Grandeur', or have responded to storm and tempest as Hopkins does in 'The Wreck of the Deutschland'. Creation to Hopkins is not the act or *Fiat* by which the world came into being, all its smallest and greatest elements cohering in one beautiful and rational design; it is an eternal act by which the love of God sustains the world in being. There is 'the dearest freshness deep down things'

> *Because the Holy Ghost over the bent*
> *World broods with warm breast and with ah! bright wings.*

The vision of the world's 'splendour and wonder', 'nature's bonfire burning on', the loving recreation of 'wet and wildness', 'weeds and wilderness', in Hopkins's poetry have a truth and a beauty beyond the range of earlier poets. And, in the religious poets of our own age, there is a sense of the pain of life, of 'the burthen of the mystery', 'the heavy and the weary weight of all this unintelligible world' that we miss in the poets of the seventeenth century. In such a poem as Edith Sitwell's 'Still falls the rain', or in David Gascoyne's sequence 'Miserere', there is a sense of a whole world in travail and pain, working out, or waiting for redemption. In every age, according to its strength and its limitations, poets have found ways to enrich our imagination by displaying, among other images of human life, an image of man as an animal that worships.